WHAT YOUR BOSS DOESN'T TELL YOU
Until It's Too Late

HOW TO CORRECT BEHAVIOR
THAT IS HOLDING YOU BACK

Robert Bramson, Ph.D.

A FIRESIDE BOOK
Published by Simon & Schuster
New York   London   Toronto   Sydney   Tokyo   Singapore

Fireside
Rockefeller Center
1230 Avenue of the Americas
New York, NY 10020

FIRESIDE and colophon are registered trademarks
of Simon & Schuster Inc.

Designed by Irving Perkins Associates
Manufactured in the United States of America

3   5   7   9   10   8   6   4   2

Library of Congress Cataloging-in-Publication Data

Bramson, Robert M.
What your boss doesn't tell you until it's too late: how to correct behavior that is holding you back/Robert Bramson.
        p.   cm.
1. Vocational guidance. 2. Self-evaluation. 3. Interpersonal re-
lations. 4. Self-management. 5. Career development. I. Title.
        HF5381.B658   1996
        650.1'3—dc20   95-35745
                        CIP

ISBN 0-684-81146-4

To Susan, who keeps growing, so I must change too.
She makes me practice what I preach.

Contents

Preface

In 1981, I wrote *Coping with Difficult People* because I couldn't find another book like it to which to refer my clients. Fifteen years later, I've had to do the same for the reciprocal problem—a practical manual on how to manage your own difficult behavior. Why so useful a topic has been ignored is a puzzle, for we are all at times at least a little difficult, and much is known about what to do about it.

There is no shortage of tomes on how to understand yourself; they presume that self-understanding automatically leads to changed behavior. It does not. There are motivational tracts that inspire you to be all you can be, texts that teach communicative and organizational skills, and, more recently, solid books and articles on how to control a variety of lifestyle problems—alcoholism and smoking, for example. But I could not find a manual on how to modify your behavior just enough to be less intimidating, indecisive, or complaining—to mention a few of the behavior flaws that I've seen derail perfectly good careers. So—once again—I was stuck with writing it. Here it is.

The approaches, steps, and methods that make up this book come largely from my experience over the past twenty years of helping others learn to deal with their own or others' difficult behavior. But that experience has been informed by infusions from many others.

My present partners, Susan Bramson and Lucy Gill, continue to provide inspiration, professional insight, and perspectives that are different enough to balance my own. Susan, also my wife, fellow parent, and frequent coconsultant, continually challenges me with her ability to see beyond surface reality to deeper emotional truths. Lucy, formerly a research associate at the Palo Alto Mental Research Institute, has pioneered the application of techniques first developed in brief systemic therapy to difficult problems in the workplace; she has helped me to broaden my own repertoire of consulting techniques.

Wilson Yandell, from whom I learned much about consulting, and my friend Walcott Beatty, emeritus professor of psychology at San Francisco State University, have both made indelible imprints on my way of thinking about people: how they often can grow and how they sometimes cannot. Although since my early student days my contacts with him have been limited, I need to say the same about James Bugental, whose books have continued to renew the richness of insight that I found in him long ago.

My thanks to editorial friend Kara Leverte for helping shape the original plan of the book, to Marilyn Abraham of Fireside Books, who has been so supportive through the years, and to my editor, Cynthia Gitter, for seeing this book through its final editorial and production phases. Carol Mann—my friend and agent for fourteen productive years—has, as usual, been there for me. She probably doesn't know the depth to which I value and appreciate that.

My children and their families have had a major part in shaping me into the person I am today, and therefore they are a part of the making of this and every other book I have written. I hope they are pleased with the products.

A note on gender usage: I have tried to avoid the awkward "she or he" or "s/he" by using the plural form or by alternating "he" or "she" when the singular form made more sense. In either case, "she" is intended to include "he," and "he" to include "she," for neither difficult behavior nor the ability to modify it is the sole province of either sex. As much as possible I've tried to describe real people in the cases and examples of the book, changing names, places, and, where it would not detract from the value of the example, the sex, organizational setting, and any other fact that might invade the privacy of the individuals involved.

Introduction: What Your Boss Doesn't Tell You Until It's Too Late

If you are supremely confident that you are never irritating, annoying, or difficult in any way, read no more—this book is not for you. For it assumes that as human beings we are all imperfect, that most of us are only partly aware of our flaws and foibles, and that—no matter how far we have advanced in our careers—our behavioral quirks can and eventually will limit the degree to which we benefit from our best and most exceptional qualities. We drag those troublesome ways behind us like invisible encumbrances until, at some place in our careers—a type of job, an organizational level, a chance for a partnership—they snag and hold us back, or we wear ourselves out trying to pull free.

Here, for example, are two attractive and able people who suddenly found themselves so snagged.

Tough-Minded Travis

It took two weeks for Travis Riddle to climb out of a black emotional hole enough to face his boss. Three important members of his community mental-health project's advisory committee had marched into Travis's office because "we want everything out in the open." Then they told him that they had just insisted to Travis's boss that he appoint a new project director. Yeah, they told Travis, he had done an okay job of setting up the counseling center, but now someone "with a broader, more flexible outlook" was needed.

Later, Travis coaxed one of his friends on the committee into admitting that for months there had been more than a little grumbling that Travis was a black-and-white thinker with only one way to do things—his way. "You're very smart, Trav, but you don't have any patience with anyone who doesn't see it your way. I tried to tell you that a few months ago, but frankly, you're not much for listening either. What I'm surprised about is that your boss hasn't been on your back about it before. Now these guys are fed up and out to get you."

Hardheaded Hildy

Hildy prided herself on being a no-nonsense, hardheaded supervisor. She was impatient with trivial talk, made decisions quickly and surely when she had to, got rid of those who couldn't measure up, and was hurt, angry, and puzzled when she was twice passed over for promotion. "They say I don't communicate well," was her plaint. "Maybe so, but my numbers are better than any other supervisor's, and that's what it's supposed to be all about."

Sometimes, as they did with Travis and Hildy, the consequences of behavioral impediments will hit you with sudden and emotionally devastating force: Your organization is restructured, and you are the first to be selected out. Or once again you're edged out of a promotion by someone whose judgment and competence are inferior to your own.

At other times, the message will be more subtly delivered: A note on your E-mail from an unidentified wag in Human Resources announces that the department you supervise has been the grand winner in the grievance sweepstakes this month. Or perhaps it's merely an office mate who tears you down in front of others—always with a laugh, of course, but you catch your best work pal glancing up to see how you're taking it.

When you've been stung by these indignities or have been told that you are sometimes overbearing, abrasive, or moody, that you may waffle, hector, or complain a bit, or that in some other ways you are difficult or hard to understand, you may simply define yourself as a loser in the personality parade, wish you were different, and lower your sights. Most of the time, however, if you are like the people with whom I've worked, you'll do something quite different. Fighting to keep your ego intact, you'll ascribe your troubles to the collection of weaklings, dummies, and goons that dog you every day, and indeed, sometimes you will be right—at least in part.

At times, in truth, your troublesome behaviors will not have mattered much, particularly when you were at beginning occupational levels where your technical competencies might overshadow any behavioral flaws. And there are always plenty of reasons for believing that it's the situations you're in and not yourself that needs fixing. Difficult bosses, vindictive customers, hard economic times, and organizational restructuring are all factors over which none of us have much control.

Sure, at times you may wonder if there might be something about yourself that deserves a second look. But even then, you might reasonably ask, shouldn't you simply accept yourself as you are and search for a place where your talents and native qualities will be better appreciated? "After all," you might think, "can't I assume my bosses, coworkers, and clients will make allowances for occasional lapses? What am I supposed to do—commit to three years on the couch to excise the troublesome parts of my personality? What about the cost in time and money? And anyway, I couldn't really be all that bad—look how far I've already come. And besides, really talented people are always a little quirky."

One alternative is to continue to ignore the warning signs until, one way or another, they exact a price that you have not consciously chosen to pay. I have seen enough clients at every organizational level react to career disappointments in this way to be convinced that it is quite the norm for ambitious careerists.

But there is another way—bolder, if less frequently taken. Identify what it is you do that annoys, irritates, and exasperates those who are important to your work success, and then learn to minimize, modify, and contain that behavior sufficiently to allow your energy and ability to take you as far as you want to go. This is a book about how to do that.

The methods and techniques that you'll find in each chapter have evolved from my twenty-five years of consulting with managers and professionals of every stripe and level who wanted—or were ordered—to get help in modifying behavioral flaws that were reducing their effectiveness or promotability. Through the years the methods have been refined and extended by my partners and valued associates, and, just as important, they are consistent with current behavioral science research.

This book, then, is for energetic and capable people like Travis and Hildy who (1) wish they didn't lose their temper, give in, cry, or turn others off; (2) have been yelled at, hinted at, fired, or passed over for promotion; (3) have been told to be more, or less, aggressive, to communicate more or less, to be less wordy and more emotional, or vice versa; or (4) have been informed of any other annoying, irritating, or discomfiting behavior that has detracted from their effectiveness. This book is not offered as a self-help form of psychotherapy. Its objective is not to change your personality but rather to facilitate a modest reduction in the nature and intensity of whatever behavior is interfering with your own best interests. On the other hand, if you are already embarked on the therapeutic adventure, what you'll find in the balance of this book can serve as useful interim measures until the motivation and irrationalities that underlie the difficult behavior have been sufficiently untangled.

In the chapters that follow, you'll find a workable approach to answering two fundamental questions: (1) How do I learn to see myself, flaws and felicities alike, through the eyes of those others—bosses, coworkers, clients, and customers—who are most important to my success? and (2) How do I—in a manner consistent with my own way of doing things and acceptable to me on moral and ethical grounds—minimize, modify, or contain my liabilities without giving up essential aspects of my personality or my self?

Even if you are not now ready to tackle such questions for yourself, consider this manual as a resource for subordinates, coworkers, or bosses to whom you wish to say—or have said— "We like, value, and respect you, but would you stop being so . . . " (If you should buy the book for someone else, however, you might want to read the first few chapters yourself. You may just decide to buy a second copy.)

In Chapter 1 we'll consider the pros and cons of making a commitment to change, along with a list of indicators that might suggest to you that a decision to move ahead would be wise.

Chapters 2 and 3 discuss specific steps for finding out how others see you, and suggest how to use the information you obtain to develop a practical plan of action.

Chapter 4 takes you step by step through a behavior-management process that enables you to get into action as boldly or unobtrusively as your circumstances require.

Chapter 5 is about recasting any negative perceptions that important people may have about you, justified or not; unfortunately, images about you may not change even though your behavior has.

In Chapters 6 to 9 you'll find a more focused look at problems and opportunities involved in managing or modifying some of the more common difficult behavior patterns. Although you may not be that kind of difficult person at all, you may get some useful ideas to pass on to those you supervise or team up with.

Chapter 10 explores the potential value for you of going deeper—entering into a longer-term change process—and suggests indicators that can tell you when it might be worth pursuing.

Readiness to change, to put aside or reshape behaviors that have been part of you, perhaps for many years, is the heart of the undertaking you are now contemplating. So understanding in some detail just how that change comes about can help you decide whether and to what extent you'll want to proceed. To that end, move on to Chapter 1.

1

Choosing to Change

Over the years, I've helped two sorts of clients modify troublesome behaviors that were getting in their way. More frequently than one might suppose, there were senior executives and professional or technical stars continually striving to better their own peak performances. For them, the major hurdle was simply coaxing others to provide feedback that ventured beyond "Everything's great, you're the best" to at least a reluctant "Well, there *are* a few things that might be a little better." While they never enjoyed the criticism, they encouraged it, because they knew it to be the only route to honing their already considerable skills.

If you see yourself in this heroic company, excelling but always seeking improvement, skip the rest of this chapter and skim succeeding chapters for suggestions on refining your self-development efforts. If you are not quite there yet, read on. For most of my clients have been highly talented people who were caught unawares by the discovery that their careers had turned sluggish or had been blocked or derailed and that they might be contributors to that derailment. The bitter portents ranged from scathing exit interviews, abysmal performance reports, and threats of dismissal with cause to repeated promotional turn-downs. Hardly any initially agreed that the faults lay in them-selves, and most could not believe that they had been so out of touch with their coworkers' perceptions of them. I encouraged them to remain skeptical as they began their investigations, but to be open to all possibilities. I encourage you to do the same. For such disagreeable events can serve several useful purposes.

First, the surprise—"shock" may be a more accurate term—of discovering just how incompletely you know how you are seen by others, especially those whose opinions are important to you, can prod you to get on with the work of identifying and then modifying your least effective behaviors. It can also help salve your ego. After all, if you were unaware that your words, ac-tions, or demeanor had made unintended impressions on others, how could you have averted the effects of those impressions?

Second, like symptoms of an illness, the direction and severity of the blows that fell can help you define just what needs fixing and what does not. For example, it was clear to Hildy, the overly aggressive manager in Section I, that her technical prowess was not in question; neither was her energy or her ability to bring in a project on time and within budget. Instead, it was her interper-sonal skills, or the seeming lack of them, that were holding her back.

Finally, and most important, hurtful as the messages are, they serve as a timely warning that unnoticed aspects of your behav-ior are blocking your progress. Heeding that warning, blatant or subtle as it sometimes is—recognizing that some of what you do or how you do it is costing you more than you've consciously chosen to pay—is the key to change.

The purpose of this chapter is to assist you in deciding whether or not dealing effectively with your own difficult behav-ior is the right course for you. Once again, stay skeptical, but keep as open as you can to possibilities.

The Journey toward Commitment to Change

"All right," Sally said to me, "so my boss told you that I'm a self-righteous, opinionated know-it-all who never listens. Tell me this, Dr. Bramson—if that's so, how come I'm the highest-paid product manager in Corporate Marketing, and I'm only thirty-three?"

"Well," I said with, I suppose, more than a touch of pomposity, "the question is, do you want to be promoted to director of marketing here or somewhere else, or is your present level okay?"

"That's another thing," she said. "Tom"—the present marketing director—"was sure a super salesman, but he still hasn't signed off on my product plan for this year—he's as indecisive as they come. Nice, but absolutely helpless unless everyone agrees. Are you really sure I'll be better off like him?"

Sally didn't know it, but she was well into the preparation phase of the change process—an uneasy awareness that something might be amiss, interspersed with energetic efforts to assuage fear, anger, or shame by proving that there is no *real* problem (everyone does it), that it's someone or something else's fault (my boss can't expect me to know everything that's going on in the division), or that you're helpless to fix it anyway (my mother always said I was too sure of myself). While others may see the need for you to change, as both Sally's boss and subordinates did, your clever defenses will keep you doggedly looking the other way.

Generally, this knack for not seeing yourself as the source of problems is rather handy. It keeps you optimistic and willing to try again, and helps you maintain a high level of performance in tight situations. (Sure, it may also add a little to your store of buried anxiety because a part of you knows that you are lying to yourself, but that's handled in another part of your resilient brain.)

You *can* stay in this "I'm fine the way I am" stage a long time, perhaps for the rest of your career. Ironically, the more competent you are at some valued skill, the less motivated you may be to tackle the behavioral problems that have limited the extent or direction of your future growth. It wouldn't be lack of will or courage that would stop you, but simply that the costs of changing might seem more than you're yet willing to pay. It would not be at all unrealistic to say—as certainly Sally did—"If I'm doing okay now, why borrow trouble? Doesn't 'If it ain't broke, don't fix it' apply to people as well as automobiles?"

That's an important and very real question—trying to change a behavioral tic that you've managed to live with for so long might not be worth the cost. To answer the question you must balance the costs of development and the consequences of doing nothing against potential gains, an important if not always an easy task. On one side are the demands and discomforts you will encounter along the way: the unpleasantness of asking for and listening to feedback from others, conflict over stealing from other tasks time that you'll need for learning, and the strain of paying attention, at least for a time, to how well you're doing. There will also be a less obvious cost to you: your sense of loss as you forgo some of the satisfactions that were part of your old habits of behaving. Let's examine some of these costs in more detail.

Time, Attention, and Strain

Like any new task, modifying a part of your behavioral inventory will take time and attention away from the other projects that fill your busy life; you'll recover some of that time by no longer being forced to clear away the debris left by your difficult behavior. How comfortable you'll be depends upon several factors: whether your sense of humor remains intact when the focus of attention is your own contradictory behavior, the degree to which you gain support from your fellows (more on this in succeeding chapters), and even whether the behavior has a partially genetic basis—the evidence is mounting that some tendencies to behave one way or another are inherited. The best example of this is aggressiveness.

Certainly, biologists have been able to breed generations of hostile, attacking rats; toreadors can attest to the special fierceness of the bulls bred for the corrida; and the evidence from studies of identical twins reared apart indicates that many such human personality characteristics are at least 50 percent inherited. Psychologist Abraham Tesser has pointed out that when attitudes have a biological substrate, they tend to be enduring, and efforts to change them will be particularly stressful. True, your goal will not be personality change, but rather the achievement of new skills, perspectives, and better control. Still, to the extent that you're fighting your own biology, you'll continually need to remind yourself that what feels right and natural may not always be in your best interest.

On the other hand, to replace an acquired behavior habit held over from another setting, because you were unaware that there were any career-adverse consequences, may require only a few moments' thought and a modicum of practice.

Change Causes Ripples

Less obvious, perhaps, is that your changed behavior will place inevitable pressures on others to give up their habitual responses to you. For example, although they had been vociferous in complaining about her demanding, know-it-all behavior, Sally's staff members were initially nonplussed because without her tight grasp on every decision, they were forced to think for themselves. Worse, they could no longer blame her for mistakes that showed up later.

Similarly, if you are an easily persuaded executive who finally learns to say "no!" your new aura of substance may please some of your colleagues, but it will just as likely discomfit others. For example, if you are now more able to disagree openly with your teammates, they will be forced to deal with your facts, opinions, and differing perspective—a genuine nuisance to them. From a broader perspective, of course, they will also benefit. While they may complain that you, who used to be so nice, are now difficult, they will be better problem solvers because they have to contend with what you have to say.

Loss of Self

Especially if you are of a somewhat introspective bent, you may be troubled by such thoughts as these: "If I stop behaving naturally and spontaneously, won't I be giving up part of myself—become just another false-faced role player? Acting differently than I feel just isn't honest." Or if you tend to be more extroverted, you might wonder if it isn't a kind of surrender of your individuality to change your behavior because others want you to.

Questions like these have often been of serious concern to clients who were struggling to stay centered while contemplating change. They are not easy to answer, because the notions that underlie these issues—such as "You should always present yourself as you really are; to wear a false front is weak and dishonest"—contain both sense and nonsense. Certainly, behaving purposefully rather than spontaneously is acting contrary to your nature, and the you who is behaving is not the real you if "real" means what came out of the original mold cast by your genes and your earliest experiences. But acting differently than you feel was one of the first things you learned; an obvious example—in almost any social setting, you do not physically hit others even though they've made you angry enough to feel like doing just that. The emotional part of your nature may be telling you to bash, but the thinking part is saying, "Not here and now."

Nonetheless, purposely behaving with artifice can be disturbing, even when the logic of it seems evident. Even tough Hildy, who grimly strode down the aisles of the manufacturing department she managed, had a hard time with the idea of practicing a slightly more agreeable facial expression in front of her home mirror. I'd suggested it because many of her staff had mistakenly interpreted her turned-down mouth as expressing unremitting disapproval of everything and everyone in sight.

She finally agreed when I pointed out that whether one's mouth turned up or down at rest was largely a genetically determined characteristic. Since she had chosen neither her parents nor their genes, I could see no reason why she had to be stuck with others' reactions to an unintended sour appearance. Further, she was not spinelessly giving in to others' objections. Rather, she had found herself in a career that required that she work with others, and she could see that their reactions affected her ability to serve her own interests. "So," she grudgingly summed up, "you're saying that I either have to work alone, figure that I'm never going to be anything but a floor boss, or learn to smile like an idiot when I'm really just thinking about how to get production higher and scrap lower." I admitted that I couldn't see any other alternatives.

But all is not lost on the "to thine own self be true" front. To paraphrase social psychologist Kenneth Gergen, you needn't give up the notion of authentic self—a way of thinking of one's being in the world—in order to see that certain ways you've taken to have made life harder for you. That realization simply becomes part of your new authentic self.

Giving Up Problem Behavior Is Also Giving Up Satisfactions

Difficult behaviors—whether or not initially pushed by our genes—become part of our repertoires because they work for us; that is, they help us satisfy some practical or psychological needs. For example, Travis's world became a little more secure every time he made others conform to his structured, highly rational plans; Hildy felt a rush as she tugged, bashed, and battered people and materials into products that unceasingly marched out the door; and Sally's sense of personal value was reaffirmed each time her expertness prevailed.

They each faced the same dilemma: when you surrender the problem, you also give up the satisfactions that came with it, a loss that may be only partially balanced by the new skills and enhanced mastery over your work life you've acquired. For, unfortunately, these worthy attainments seldom match the pure pleasure that follows a high-decibel scathing indictment of a sinner. As Sally put it toward the end of our time together, "Since I started listening more and experting less, my staff is really working as a team—we make fewer mistakes—and our idea-to-product time is way down. But somehow I'm not getting the buzz that I used to get when I was the department guru. It's like with my diet. I like feeling slim and fit, but it's sure no substitute for a double hot-fudge sundae."

There is, however, a perspective that can sustain you in those moments when you wonder whether a more effective persona is worth your surrendering the pleasures that accrue from bullying, experting, gaining peace by sidestepping conflict, or whatever other problem behaviors you're thinking of modifying. Keep in mind that your task is to change how you *use* your motivations, which is well within your control, not how to rid yourself of them, which is not at all possible anyway. To shift your coworkers' view of you from "abrasive" to "forceful but supportive" doesn't require that you stop wanting to feel powerful and influential, merely that you channel those wishes differently. Here you are aided by one of the more felicitous ironies of being human: your behavioral liabilities often stem from the very motives and qualities that are your most valuable.

For example, Sally's pride in her incisive mind was not merely inflated ego. Her insight and decisiveness had real and obvious value for herself, her unit, and her organization. However, her confidence in *her* right answer often made it difficult for her to see that other paths to the same goal might be equally—well, almost equally—right.

"It's hopeless then," was Sally's first response when I pointed out that her problem was largely that she was a little too strong-minded, "because my way usually does seem to be the best, and there isn't always time to get into all the other possibilities. On the other hand, you're saying that I don't really have to change my personality or my way of doing things, maybe just ease up a little. That way I can still use my brains—just make sure I'm listening to what others have to say first. Have I got the idea?"

"Mostly," I proffered, knowing it would not be quite as simple as that but not wanting to quench her enthusiasm. "Certainly no one wants to see you stop using your brain."

What If I Choose Not to Change?

As your final task in deciding whether or not to move ahead, you need to balance the costs of changing against the consequences of doing nothing.

Sometimes the consequences will be obvious. For Nate, a store owner and operator who constantly promised his customers levels of service that couldn't be met, the consequences of not modifying his behavior were complaints, customer ill will, and a business that should have been, but wasn't, growing. For Sally, an obvious consequence of not amending her management style was not getting promoted to marketing director, a position she wanted and felt she deserved. Paradoxically, obvious and serious consequences like these help make the decision for you. Although the messages are highly unpleasant to receive, words or actions that tell you that "things aren't going well" simplify the job of weighing costs, benefits, and consequences.

However, when the signs that some behavior makeover might be wise have been only fleeting thoughts of your own, hints from colleagues, or a slight slowdown in your movement through the organization's chairs, the costs of staying as you are may seem much less obvious. Perhaps at the moment you are in a relatively steady state—busy, with no organizational ripples coming your way—and the consequences of settling for less than some theoretical best future seem hazy. Even so, a careful and candid look, balancing the consequences of not changing your behavior against the benefits of doing so, may prevent regrets or resentful complaining later in your career.

From time to time I have been able to stay in touch with highly competent people who chose not to follow a developmental path. Sometimes it was just that the path was wrong or that the time for change was not yet at hand. An acquaintance named Mark comes to mind. He was a personable midcareer salesman who, after resisting repeated urgings that he undertake advanced sales training, found his real calling as a master high school teacher. For Rita, an assistant corporate treasurer, it was a matter of her own readiness. She turned down her company's offer of developmental coaching and then, at her own expense, retained me for the same purpose four years later.

But there were also more than a few people who chose not to make the commitment to change, only to regret that choice later. The case of Jill Barlow, an experienced and successful marketing consultant, is particularly puzzling, because she had been ready for change at one point in her career, but not at another, although the benefits to her might have been equally great.

A substantial part of Jill's income came from technical consultations, initially to heads of marketing departments and later to senior managers who wanted to assess their overall marketing strategy. The balance of her income—and it was growing—derived from the lecture/seminar circuit, where I met her.

Once, when we were relaxing at cocktails, both of us having made presentations to a rather testy audience, she confessed that soon after her start as a speaker she had been crushed by audience evaluations of her presentation skills: she wrung her hands, she spoke in a monotone, she "moved like a robot."

After a temporary period of withdrawal and depression, she had enrolled in a public-presentation class and, in addition, had sought coaching from colleagues who were willing to help her out. Her speaking career had then blossomed, and she had spent the last six years as busy as she wanted to be, giving seminars and doing workshops at a variety of association meetings.

But now, she told me she was aware of receiving what seemed like subtle feedback from several colleagues and even from those who were hiring her to speak. "Have you thought of using humor more?" her clients asked. "Have you thought of joining the National Speaker's Association, where you'll have a wonderful opportunity to speak and get evaluated?" one of her colleagues had asked.

She was, she said, really resentful of him, and told me that not only didn't she need that kind of coaching ("Why, last week I got raves!") but in fact she found the members of the association he wanted her to join too shallow; and besides, she was just too busy. Yet toward the end of our conversation, her guard lowered a bit; perhaps, by the informal setting and the libations, she asked me, a bit plaintively, just how one wangled invitations to keynote at the president's forums that crowned the meetings of industry associations.

Some months later, I heard more from Walt, the very colleague who had suggested that she open herself to a new round of feedback. He had given up trying to help Jill out. "I really feel bad about it, Bob," he said. "Several times I've suggested her as a speaker at one of the top-level meetings that I couldn't make, the ones that really pay the big bucks, and each time she's disappointed the meeting sponsors. The fact is that when everything is going right and the audience is hot for her topic, she goes over very well. But those times don't occur often. To really be at the peak in this racket, you've got to come through even when things are going against you. The sad part is that I'm sure with a little more voice training and some expert coaching, Jill could have been another Terry Clausen [one of America's top management speakers]. But, much as I like her, she won't get another referral from me."

I next had a chance for a real conversation with Jill some years later, just before she was retiring from speechmaking. She was obviously pleased that she had achieved some standing as an expert in her field and helped many to do their jobs better. But it still ate at her that she had not achieved the top echelon of motivational speakers. Had she remembered the decision she had made not to reenter the developmental path?

"Maybe I should have listened to Walt a few years back," she finally ventured, "but I kept thinking that with a little more effort and time I'd finally make it on my own."

Perhaps that was it, but maybe she had simply recalled her past experience, distastefully anticipating further rounds of critical comment, the superior attitudes of "helpful" coaches, and the awkwardness of "trying more humor" than was natural for her. She had found a style that worked well enough. Would it have been worth it just to attain some sort of perfection that might be out of her reach anyway?

Clearly the point here is not whether Jill had a right to settle for what she had already attained—she had a reasonable measure of occupational success; she was doing well. But would she have made that same choice if she had been able to foresee the depth of her future regret? Jill's experience seems to bear out the value of an approach suggested by psychologists Twersky and Kahneman, who have carefully studied the anatomy of wrong decisions: to test out any important decision, they say, ask yourself, "If I act as this decision tells me to, how will I feel now and in the future?" That, of course, is the final question to put to yourself as you contemplate whether to move ahead, hold your ground, or fall back to a safer, less demanding occupational goal.

DO I REALLY NEED TO MAKE A COMMITMENT TO CHANGE?

What follows is a compendium of many of the events that have warned clients that career hazards over which they might have some control lay in their path. You may want to think of it as a checklist. If you find yourself faced with more than two of these indicators, take a closer look.

- Has there been a change in management philosophy or in the criteria by which your behavior is evaluated? For example, has a management that formerly supported a family feeling in the company been displaced by reengineering-minded or cost-conscious senior executives? These new bottom-line managers seem to show little tolerance for marginal performers and even less for the well-intentioned supervisors (you?) who believe in giving everyone a chance to improve.

- Have you changed your job, perhaps through promotion, only to find that the qualities on which the change was based—often those of which you're most proud—don't fit of the requirements of the new job?

- Are you a senior-level professional or manager in a field with a rapidly expanding knowledge and skill base, but you are not keeping up?

- Do you have a new boss who has not fully communicated her expectations but now seems disappointed when you perform in what was formerly a satisfactory fashion?

- Have you been passed over for a promotion to a job for which you were technically qualified? Disregard the fact that you have been given reasonable explanations as to why you were not selected ("It was a very close thing, but we picked George because he had a little more experience with overseas customers"). Often behavioral flaws tolerated at a lower level, where technical abilities are judged to be more important, become barriers to promotion to higher levels, where all candidates have satisfactory technical prowess and other considerations, such as creativity, interpersonal skills, and negotiation ability, become the deciding factors. Be especially alert to this possibility if you find yourself twice passed over and you or others chalk it up to politics.

- Are assignments you expected given to others, particularly when dealing with people is involved?

- Do you find yourself frequently left out of important information loops or informal influence networks; for example, do you find out about important events, even those that affect your work, only through official communications or formal staff meetings?

- When you ask questions about the quality of your performance, do you often get evasive or indirect answers ("You're pretty much doing what we need you to do")?

- While generally satisfactory, have your performance reports contained consistent comments that you are less than adequate in certain areas? (These areas may not have been really discussed with you, or you may have ignored them because they are peripheral to your job, and besides, most likely your boss's assessment is incorrect anyway.)

- Is your performance level adversely affected by severe stress at work or at home? Remember that stressful conditions tend to foster excessive use of your strongest qualities and at the same time diminish your ability to notice changes in your own behavior or in the reactions of others.

- Are you the butt of frequent kidding remarks about your behavior or your performance from your boss or coworkers? Such joshing is commonplace in many settings, and among males is one form of permitted intimacy. Key questions are: Do the acknowledged stars in the group also receive their share of kidding? Are the comments said in jest similar to the comments you've received in a more serious tone from the boss or colleagues?

- Do you find yourself frequently explaining away negative comments about your performance; for instance, reasoning

your boss out of a criticism that's been made or patiently
pointing out why you didn't produce expected results?

- Do you frequently feel out of touch with the goals and priorities of your organization, as if you are the only wise, astute, smart one, surrounded by fools?

- Do peers sometimes make sincere but possibly double-
  edged comments about you or your work, such as, "I really
  like working with you; you always seem to have the right
  answers"?

If you've decided that your behavior warrants a deeper look,
your first task will be to get more information so you won't end
up solving the wrong problem in the wrong way. Chapter 2 out-
lines a step-by-step approach for discovering precisely what it is
you need to change.

2

Sizing Up the
Task and Setting
Your Targets

All right, you've accepted the possibility that, to some as yet un-known degree, you may be inadvertently impeding your own progress. Your next step is to find out as specifically as possible just what you are doing that lessens your value to important others. That sort of detective work is less daunting if you do it one step at a time, tackling, in roughly this order, each of the following tasks: (1) Look for clues to others' reactions to you in past experiences that you might have paid little attention to or even dismissed; (2) sharpen your objectivity by reviewing what's known about how easy it is to misread what others really think of you; (3) observe yourself in action for a time without making any changes at all; (4) select the most likely prospects to mine for more infor-mation; (5) carry out conversations with them; and, finally, (6) use what you've discovered to set feasible developmental goals.

LOOKING FOR CLUES

"I can't believe that they said I never listen to them," declared Sally incredulously. "I always wait until they've told me their side of the story before I say anything."

"No one else has said anything like that to you, then?" I countered.

There was a silence as Sally stared first at me and then at the summarized comments of her colleagues that were spread on the desk in front of her.

"Well," she finally said, "when I got this job—it was quite a promotion for me—my old boss said something about my learning to communicate better, but I thought he was talking about my making presentations, so I took a course in public speaking and joined Toastmasters. Why would he say I needed to communicate better if he really meant that I needed to be"—she stopped and grabbed one of the pages, scanning for the right comment—"'less positive about everything'?"

There was another long pause as Sally again stared unseeing at the papers on her desk. "I wonder if that's what my husband means when he says I'm opinionated."

"Are there other things that you can remember that might relate to 'less positive' or 'not listening to what others have to say'?" I asked. "Has anything like that ever come out in your performance reviews?"

"I don't think so," she replied. "Just a moment and we'll see." She opened her file drawer and pulled out copies of her last two performance reports, put one in front of her and handed the other to me. There it was on page two, under general comments:

> You are an intelligent and highly professional asset to our department. I particularly value the decisiveness you've shown in carrying out often difficult assignments involving the public and highly placed political figures. However, as I have mentioned to you in the past, I have noticed that you have sometimes appeared to ignore both facts and opinions that others see as being of importance. On occasion I have even noticed that in our one-on-one briefing sessions. This might be a significant problem and deserves your attention.

When I passed it over to Sally, she immediately flipped the performance report she was perusing to page two, frowned a bit, neatly folded page one back, and handed it to me. It was the identical paragraph.

"Anything else you can think of?" I asked.

"Well," she said, "when I was in college, I had this big falling-out with my roommate, who called me a smart-ass know-it-all and said that I would never have any friends. Of course, I had just called her a stupid bubblehead because she had thrown out six months of my library notes, and anyway, by the end of the semester we were back to being friends. Are you saying that I should have taken all these things seriously? You know, if my boss really cares about what he put in the performance report, he would say something about it. All I get from him is how competent I am and how happy he is that I really produce. On the other hand, the reason that you and I are here together is that he's told me that if I wanted to get promoted again, I'd better work with you on improving my interpersonal skills, whatever that means. Does that mean that I'm supposed to take every negative that anyone ever throws at me as being the gospel? I just don't believe it."

Sally certainly had a point. People often lambast others with derogatory comments because they feel hurt, anxious, or insecure, or are simply in a wretched mood. After all, wasn't Sally's "stupid bubblehead" remark just an expression of her frustration over yet another weekend of library note taking, not a reasoned judgment about her roommate's intelligence? And isn't much of what passes for criticism merely an outpouring of the critic's own prejudgments and self-serving biases?

To be sure. Yet, distorted or not, the allegations of others, shouted, whined, or disguised as they often are, usually contain some truth. Even those irksome evaluations can be the start and foundation of the most valuable kind of learning: how to make the most effective use of your most important instrument—yourself. To be convinced of the need to attend to, even encourage, that sort of negative feedback and yet to stay reasonably clearheaded, you'll need to feel fully in your bones the subtle ways in which, without knowing it, you can be out of touch with how you are seen and judged by others. Here, then, is a summary of what we know about the mischievous processes that keep us from seeing what we need to see. As you read through it, try to assess for yourself the degree to which any of these normal human attributes may have prevented you from accurately assessing how others react to you.

Why We Misread Others' Views of Ourselves

The question of how well people read others' perceptions of them has long intrigued students of human behavior, so we have some answers to the puzzle of why people like Sally are blind to just what they most need to see. Actually, there are several good reasons why it couldn't be any other way.

Our Creative Perceptions

For one thing, there is the creativity of human perception and memory. Studies have consistently shown that our feelings, wishes, and desires—that complexity of self-interests that we commonly call *ego*—profoundly influence the way we see the world and everything in it. We are more storytellers than mere recorders of what is actually out there. Having perceived things in our own way, we then diligently apply our intelligence to make our distortions plausible, and it's easy to see why the brightest people often put themselves in harm's way, not bravely, but in ignorance that they are doing so.

We Read the Group Well, but Individuals Poorly

Perhaps it is this perceptual malleability that explains a puzzling contradiction in studies of how well we know how our associates really see us. Let's say we ask Ted, your average office worker, to guess how each one of his office mates might rate him on a number of characteristics. We also ask each one of his mates individually to rate him on the same characteristics. Then we take an average of Ted's and his office mates' ratings. If we compare the *average* of Ted's guesses with the *average* of his associates' actual ratings, we find them so close that we assure him that all is well—he won't be in for any surprises.

Then, however—curious about why Ted seems, obliviously, to keep ruffling the feathers of the very people he wants to think well of him—we compare his guesses about how he's seen by each *individual* coworker with the individuals' actual ratings of him, and we find the awful truth: while his guesses are quite on the money in some cases, they're way off the mark in others.

Many of his coworkers do see him as competent, if modest and unassuming. This pleasant generalization wouldn't be a problem if it were not also true, although Ted is quite unaware of it, that although his assistant believes him to be the finest professional he's ever known, his boss has marked him as rather ordinary, plodding, and unimaginative. Nor will he likely find out differently, since he's confident of his standing, and with good reason—hasn't he correctly intuited the overall opinion of his work group? So he has little reason to pay much attention to the subtle clues that might tell him otherwise.

Ted will be further confounded by his wish that his boss think as well of him as he thinks of himself—at least on good days— and he will blind himself to the hesitations, sudden silences, and unimaginative assignments that might have led him to wonder. When the senior-level promotion goes, for the second time, to other, more visibly creative people, the odds are, as we shall next see, that Ted, being a normal human being, will blame it all on politics, favoritism, or some other cause removed from himself.

From the Inside Things Look Different Than They Do from the Outside

Adding to the confusion is the likelihood that while you tend see your behavior as a reasonable response to what's happening around you, your associates will interpret your behavior as the result of *who* you are, often characterizing it in their minds as "just like you." In fact, both perspectives are to some extent correct: what you do at any given time largely results from your balancing the requirements of the situation with your tendency to act consistently across all situations (which we call personality). The point is that you and your coworkers tend to focus on different sides of this equation, thus setting the stage for problems, especially when things go wrong.

Next we turn to a seeming paradox—some have called it the awful irony of being human—that your liabilities are often nothing more than your strengths inappropriately or excessively applied.

The Strength-Weakness Paradox

Let's say your boss has openly accused you of being inflexibly rigid. You might, with equal truth, aver that you are not at all rigid, but are instead steadfast, gritty, and unwaveringly persevering. "Rigid" and "steadfastly persevering" are, in fact, two manifestations of the same thing, namely the quality of maintaining one's position in the face of difficulty. If there is a difference, it is primarily one of degree.

The notion that too much of a good thing can create problems is certainly not new. Moreover, recent studies of decision making and interpersonal influence have helped specify just how and why competent people misapply their best qualities to achieve the worst results. Take the quality of aggressiveness, just what is needed to make someone active and forceful, a real go-getter, a confident producer of results. Use that same desirable quality excessively, however, and "active" becomes "pushy," forcefulness becomes bullying, and confident decisiveness turns into arrogant single-mindedness.

Often the behavioral distance between just enough and too much is rather small—an added reason why you and others may differ in your evaluations. For example, twice I saw and heard Hildy, the hardheaded manufacturing manager from Section I, bluntly and without the prescribed complimentary sandwiching (praise, drop the bomb, more praise) tell subordinates why errors they'd made were the results of poor planning. It was cold, unvarnished, and unsympathetic, but the recipients took it well, albeit rather sheepishly. (One of them later told me, "At least with her you know where you stand, and she doesn't hold grudges.") Later, she interrupted our consulting session to take a return phone call from a purchasing manager who had ignored her quality criteria when ordering a part. She restated exactly what she wanted from him and ended the conversation with, "If it happens again, Fred, I'll have your ass on the ground." As far as I know, Fred did not report her plain speaking to either his boss or hers and never again changed the specifications on her purchase orders without first consulting her.

In both of these incidents, she was tough and aggressive, yet neither trait seemed to be unfitting given the players and the situation. In contrast, I was told by her boss that he had twice seen her publicly ridiculing a junior technician for suggesting a technical change, and that she repeatedly used raw sarcasm as a tool for keeping people on their toes. Clearly she was both the tough but fair person she saw herself to be *and* the harsh and abrasive tyrant described by her boss and some, but not all, of her subordinates.

To further complicate matters, some people don't give much thought to the possibility that they might be judging themselves against criteria quite different from those held by their bosses and others who are important to the success of their work. For Hildy, as a measure of her managerial performance, superior production far outweighed hurt feelings and an occasional grievance. She was certainly correct that her bosses were mightily pleased by her high production figures, but her assumption was wrong that they did not hold interpersonal skills equally important, especially in a possible candidate for a promotion to the next level of middle management. It is not hard to see why she was so confused when promotions did not come her way.

So there are a number of reasonable and well-supported explanations of why you and your boss or colleagues may have formed quite different impressions of you, even though you have all experienced the same behavior. But that still leaves hanging the question of what may have prevented you from seeing the signs, obvious or subtle, verbal and nonverbal, that they were not satisfied with important aspects of your performance. Several all too human qualities probably explain it pretty well: like most people, you don't like to hear bad news; as an intelligent human being, you have a repertoire of fancy techniques for *not* paying much attention to it when it arrives; and there are usually a few "helpful" colleagues who will assist you in this avoidance.

Don't Upset Me with the Facts

We all have ideal images of ourselves—the person we would like to be or at least think we should be. Sure, that image is constantly jarred—by that sideways glance in the mirror, by less than ideal performances and achievements—but though beleaguered by constant contradictions from without and within, your ideal self continues to plug away at trying to make you live up to its sometimes unrealistically high standards and it has an excellent weapon for doing just that: it can make you anxious. When thoughts, feelings, or your behavior tell you things are not what they should be, you are zapped by a twinge in your diaphragm, an achy head, a spasming back muscle, or simply an awful feeling of impending doom.

Of course, it doesn't quite work out that way. Instead of punishing the wayward behavior and therefore preventing its recurrence, the well-placed jolts of anxiety reinforce a lesson most of us have learned too well: if you let yourself pay attention to hints that you are not behaving ideally, you will hurt.

Not surprisingly, your mind has developed two first-rate defenses against your ideal self's harsh treatment of you—actually, one defense with two faces: denial and blame. These defensive ploys work either by casting doubt on the indications that you're not all that you want, should, and expect to be, or, as we have seen, by imputing the causes of whatever you did to others.

Denying that facts are as they are can be done simply or with embellishments. Denials I have heard from intelligent and highly placed people range from "No, I don't do that" to those elaborate rationalizations sometimes referred to as "explaining it away," such as "Yes, I do use sarcasm when people make mistakes, because then they remember what they did wrong—and anyway, it keeps them on their toes." The special magic of this highly rational form of disaffirmation is that, by denying the premise that "your sarcasm distresses your employees," you also preclude having to deal with the conclusion that "that's why they don't tell you about mistakes."

Blaming others when problems arise probably evolved innocently enough from the natural tendency to view your behavior in a problematic situation differently from the inside than others do from the outside. Blaming certainly solves the feedback problem nicely, but unfortunately, this tendency can lead you to a too rosy view of your standing with others. Visualize you, your boss, and your colleagues mulling over a recent glitch in your part of the enterprise. They are likely to attribute the mishap to, say, your rigidity (or to the downside of whatever other personality characteristic you display most prominently). To you, however, it will be equally obvious that you were not at all rigid but rather had firmly pursued a proper course in a situation that had gone awry. If you were guilty of anything, you think to yourself, it was misjudgment—a permissible human error, not a character flaw—soon to be forgotten. When you and your group meet to debrief the disaster, and they hint, suggest, or scream that it was your inflexibility that caused the problem, you will patiently explain to them that because of their intellectual limitations, they just don't fully understand what happened. They, in turn, will bemoan your defensiveness, all too often when you're not around.

To be fair, this tendency to blame others or the situation sometimes has a quite salutary result, even though its cost is missing out on a clearer picture of how people you care about see you. Psychologist Martin Seligman has pointed out that blaming our misfortunes on circumstances outside ourselves enables us optimistically to return to the fray after one of life's many blows. As Seligman's research has demonstrated, those who respond to misfortune in this overly confident way have more successes than those who attribute the downturns to their own shortcomings, simply because they keep trying. Consoling yourself with, "Lost this sale because of a stubborn, resistant customer; next time I'll be luckier," may grant you confidence at the cost of learning from your mistakes, but since luck does play a large part in all human affairs, the next customer might just be so eager to buy that your faulty reasoning won't matter.

There is a clear contradiction between Seligman's findings and those of such peak-performer investigators as Charles Garfield. He found that optimal achievers are characterized by a high receptivity to personal feedback, especially negative feedback, seeing it as a necessary ingredient of personal learning and skill improvement. Garfield suggests, as do others' findings and my work in executive coaching, that the leavening agent is the depth and quality of the self-confidence (or sense of their own efficacy) of these high performers. In other words, the more you begin to see yourself as essentially a solid person who's picked up some problematic but modifiable attributes along the way, the less you'll need to either ignore disagreeable data or beat yourself up as an incurable sad sack.

The most practical lesson from these aggregate findings is that, while finding out about the effects of your behavior is not as simple as you might wish, it can be done. To the extent that your ideal self includes a person who is always learning and becoming more effective, you will be able to move beyond the defensive tricks your mind has invented to keep you ignorant but happy.

Take a More Objective Look at Yourself

Your first step will be to review your past for clues and commonalities.

Review the Past for Clues and Commonalities

Identifying your rough areas can be irksome, so you might as well start off with the most disagreeable task: recalling the critical performance reviews and the jibes of sniping, scathing, or sullen bosses, colleagues, or subordinates. Your purpose is not to accept that assortment of chidings as truly descriptive. You will make allowance for the 80 percent that were due to ire, envy, or upset stomachs. Then you will sift through what remains for commonalities—the same or similar comments that, in the fullness of your own self-confidence, you may have dismissed, ignored, or explained away. The end product will be a brief list of behaviors that just might be causing you more trouble than you thought.

Sally's list began this way:

- Those two performance reports said that I don't pay attention to others' ideas or objections.

- I think I give my staff plenty of time to talk, but two have remarked—one joke, one blast—that they don't think I'm listening.

- My husband has accused me of being completely rigid once my mind is made up. It's always been when we've argued and I've won, but maybe . . .

At this point, you might be tempted to say, "Wait a minute, if I've known all this before, why haven't I done anything about it?" The answer is that you didn't really *know* anything before. You had merely heard a lot of ragtag accusations or incomprehensible hints that you treated with the contempt, blaming, and denial that they seemed to deserve. The difference is that now you're paying a special kind of attention to information that was formerly background noise. You are like a detective who once again examines evidence previously ignored, this time paying close attention to details and searching for underlying themes. Keep in mind that a strength used too much, inappropriately, or without skill, will still elicit a sense of mastery and satisfaction, and therefore it is the parts of you that you are most proud of that may have led you astray.

Having completed your own sober, if unpleasant, assessment, and with the possibilities that you have uncovered in mind, you're now ready for the next step—taking some time to observe yourself in action.

Observe Yourself in Action

Some people are more self-reflective than others, tending to spend a lot of time puzzling over their own behavior. If you are one of these, this task will be a natural extension of something you do all the time.

The more outgoing and action oriented, however, are usually so preoccupied with what's going on outside themselves that they have little patience or opportunity for evaluating what's already happened: for the more extroverted it may seem like uselessly marking time when there's real work to be done. Even so, when you're trying to identify behavioral glitches, paying purposeful attention to what you do and how you do it for a week or two can be helpful in two ways.

First, it will help you move beyond any remaining bits of denial that your ego has conjured up. Witnessing her know-it-all self in action was evidently a necessary condition for Sally's commitment to change. In the face of pointed comments in two consecutive performance reports, a direct ultimatum from her boss, confirmation from my conversations with her associates, and her husband's "Well, sort of . . . " response to her "Do I really . . . ?" she still doubted that there was anything *seriously* wrong with the way she related to her staff. It was only when she noticed herself impatiently dismissing a trusted subordinate's point even before she had heard it that she was able to move ahead to plan a remedial program.

Second, if you spot a few instances in which your suspected behavioral imperfections, significant or trivial, were witnessed by your boss, colleagues, or friends, those incidents can provide solid basis for feedback on specific and recent occurrences in later conversations with those who witnessed it.

In your week of observation, think of yourself as a behavioral scientist observing that most interesting of subjects, you. Listen to the sound of your voice in meetings, in one-on-one briefings with others, in any of those settings that your personal assessment suggested are slippery slopes for you. Is it true that when a question is asked you are *always* the first with an answer? Or, having grandly announced that you are a team player, do you find yourself looking busy when an overloaded teammate silently appeals for help? You may find it helpful to count the number of times you have detected a superior tone to your voice or in other ways behaved inappropriately. Ignore as irrelevant whether the targets of your behavior deserved what they got, because that isn't the point. The point is that you are trying to get an accurate fix on how and when your behavior is having unintended effects and therefore robbing you of your effectiveness.

Having convinced yourself that further work—or at least a second look—is indicated, your next step is to size up your coworkers as sources for specific and accurate feedback.

SELECTING THE MOST LIKELY PROSPECTS FOR USEFUL FEEDBACK

From a practical standpoint, your sources for candid, coherent feedback are likely to be limited. First, they must have had ample opportunities to see you in action. Second, they must be willing. Third, you must be willing to ask them. Fourth, it's often hard to get the kind of feedback you need, even from those whose job it is to give it to you, namely your bosses.

When I have surveyed senior managers about the performance of lower-level supervisors, the most consistently cited problem, second only to poor interpersonal skills, has been inability to take corrective action with poor performers. Digging deeper, I was not too surprised to find that most of those supervisors admitted their reluctance to give direct feedback to others, even when they acknowledged their responsibility to do so. To evade the conflict between duty and their deeply felt reluctance to confront, they often hinted that a change might be helpful or couched the messages in such vague terms that the recipients were unsure just what had been said.

Hildy, for example, was told several times that she should communicate better with her subordinates. That was true enough, but it was not an adequate substitute for "Your sarcasm and public ridicule of your subordinates are having these adverse effects, and if you don't change your behavior, you will not be promoted."

In contrast, about 20 percent of those I've studied had no trouble giving direct and candid feedback. But their manner was so heavy handed—accusing, belittling, withholding support—that those on the receiving end heard it as a complete distortion or were so traumatized that they could hardly listen at all. This doesn't mean that your boss *can't* be an excellent source of feedback, just that many will need more careful preparation than you believe they should. More on that later.

Here are some possibilities to consider as sources of information:

- Peers, especially those with whom you work at least occasionally, are possible prospects. Although you may initially shy away from considering them for fear of seeming insecure or because they are potential competitors for scarce promotions, you may still be able to identify some whom you would be willing to approach, given the right conditions (say, at an off-site planning meeting). The main criterion for the first cut should be the extent to which they've been witnesses to the behavior you're trying to learn more about.

- Those you supervise are mines of information, which they *may* give you if they feel safe and supported. The key to opening staff up for productive feedback is their belief that you are ready to acknowledge that their *perceptions* are valid data in their own right. That is, the fact that they *see you* as indecisive and waffling, for example, needs to be understood and acted on, even if you are certain that you are neither. Try to encourage matter-of-fact reporting, in which your staff neither absolves you of guilt—because they like you, difficult or not—nor expresses their frustration with overdrawn, angry accusations.

- Internal or contract consultants—Human Resources staff, organizational or marketing consultants, for example—although they may have less opportunity to observe you consistently, can be both more objective and more supportive because they are less dependent on your favor. They can also assemble information about you by interviewing your boss, colleagues, subordinates, and even clients or customers, offering confidentiality to them and summarized data to you.

- If you use an internal consultant for this purpose (or if the external consultant was retained by your boss), check on any limits on the consultant's ability to keep the results of the interviews confidential. For example, Human Resources personnel sometimes feel a dual commitment to support staff *and* to keep senior management informed. In my experience, they will usually be candid about this if asked, but will not volunteer the information.

- Your bosses, of course, are paid to provide you with both positive and negative feedback, so asking them to do so is certainly a possibility, but there may be some hindrances. They may believe that they have already done their job by mentioning a few problems in your performance report or in passing on "a few things to think about," both of which actions may have received from you the scant attention they then seemed to deserve. Some bosses may, in fact, have limited opportunity to directly observe you going about your everyday business, so their feedback is based on reports from others melded with the inferences they've drawn from your versions of what happened.

- Other things being equal, coworkers whom you also think of as friends might well be the first on your list of possible sources of feedback. Your conversations will be imbedded in longer-term relationships, in which a reasonable level of trust has been built. Consider past experiences in which your friends attempted to be honest and direct with you. Were they gently trying to tell you some uncomfortable truths, perhaps too gently and with a mitigating smile? Now you can refocus that conversation with a new understanding of what they were trying to do.

- Many friends will need special permission to be honest. Because they like you, their most immediate concern may be to reassure you; however, this is precisely what you don't need, since it's likely to support your own secret hope that distorted perceptions or unfortunate circumstances are to blame for any cruel things others have said about you. Keeping the pitfalls of that sort of seductive collusion in mind will help you emphasize your need for objectivity.

It is not only your friends who may be initially reluctant to openly discuss true feelings about your behavior; many other coworkers—bosses included—may not be very forthcoming at all. There are many reasons:

- They believe you are already aware of the troublesome aspects of your behavior but just can't help behaving that way because it's part of your personality.

- They think that you're intentionally difficult to gain an advantage. For example, they believe that you yell at people because it shuts down opposition. Whether or not they are right about your motivation, they are wrong that you also chose the career damage that is the unplanned result.

- They think you should provide your own feedback, because that's what they believe they do. Their thoughts go something like, "I don't need someone else to tell me how I'm behaving; I'm well aware of what I do," and they actually believe it.

- They believe that each person has a right to behave as he or she chooses. So, since you've chosen to behave the dubious way you do, who are they to suggest that you change?

- They are well aware of negative aspects of your behavior, but because they are perhaps a little too sympathetic to others, they are reluctant to say anything that might distress you, disappoint you, or in any other way make you uncomfortable.

- They are afraid that if they point out your shortcomings, you make dislike them, and they have strong needs to be liked and accepted by others.

- They don't know what to tell you because they haven't really thought much about the specifics of your troublesome behavior, although they do react emotionally, especially when it's directed toward them. For example, they repeatedly feel irritated by your superior attitude, but they haven't thought much about what you do that produces that feeling.

- They have already accused you of being arrogant or complained about your proclivity to put off decisions, and they confuse accusation and complaining with providing useful feedback. Having told you what's wrong with you once, they don't see any reason to do it again.

- They have hinted, teased, or generalized somewhere in the neighborhood of your flawed behavior and are sure you must have gotten the point. For example, your boss has said to you in passing, "I think it's always a good idea to query staff before changing a procedure," when she really meant, "You're acting as if yours is the only possible way to do anything, and I've been hearing complaints from staff that you never listen to their ideas." However, since she thinks she has delivered the message once, she's afraid that a repetition would be viewed as nagging.

- They are simply reluctant to get involved.

While this list of barriers to candid feedback may seem discouraging initially, and it's certainly worthwhile to try for candidates who are susceptible to only a few of them, it's usually possible to coax useful information from anyone who will agree to have a conversation with you. In most cases, taking the right approach will get the results you need. To do this, you'll need a bit of mental preparation and a plan for what you'll do and say once the conversations start.

Carry Out Conversations with Your Informants

Before you start your information-gathering process, take the time to think through how you will approach your informants. Ignoring this step can lead to unnecessary frustrations and may discourage you from continuing your search. That certainly was Hildy's experience.

Plan Ahead Before You Begin

This is how Hildy characterized her first attempt to discover what it was about her no-nonsense approach that others saw as abrasive. She was talking with Rod, her longtime coffee buddy, a manager in her division's Instrument Shop. The setting was a corner table in the company cafeteria.

> Hildy: They're pressuring me about being too hard on my subordinates. You've seen me in action, Rod. Do I come on too strong sometimes?
>
> Rod (cautiously): It sounds like they're really getting to you.
>
> Hildy: You'd think that meeting production goals on time and in budget would be enough for these characters, but they say I don't relate well enough, whatever that means.
>
> Rod (with emphasis): I can't believe they want you to let up on production. Maybe they mean you don't have enough meetings.
>
> Hildy (trying again): Well, you've been in plenty of meetings with me, do you see anything wrong with the way I come across?
>
> Rod (slowly): You always know your stuff, Hildy. Sometimes

you get a little carried away, but given some of the jokers you have to deal with, I don't wonder about that. Maybe it was just bad luck about those promotions. I've got to go anyway.

HILDY: Okay, Rod. Sure. Thanks anyway.

When Hildy told me about this frustrating interaction with Rod, I found it difficult to withhold from her the fact, told to me in confidence by the division general manager, that it was Rod's cheerfully worded but essentially negative opinion of her that had led to a veto of her promotion. What I could do was help her to see that the approach she used was more likely to add to the muddle than to produce useful information.

For one thing, the setting was one in which both were accustomed to social chitchat rather than confidential and businesslike discussions. In addition, she had distanced herself from the fact-finding process by focusing the conversation entirely on "them." Worse, she had done little to assure Rod that she not only wanted the truth but could take it even if it was unflattering.

Finally, because she wasn't aware of how a friend's ambivalence can muddy a well-intentioned message, Hildy missed the clue that Rod might have more to say. "You always know your stuff, Hildy. Sometimes you get a little carried away . . . ," he'd said. A simple "Tell me more about how I sometimes get carried away, Rod" might have been enough to tip Rod toward the honest feedback that, at least in part, he wanted to give.

To avoid a discouraging start, consider the following before you begin each of your conversations:

- What's the best way to get together with this person? Do you need an appointment, or is this someone you see regularly in one-on-one discussions?

- What's the best setting for the meeting? Given your own personality and that of your informant, would a more or a less formal setting be conducive to a matter-of-fact discussion? Often a neutral site such as a conference room will provide the most relaxed atmosphere. In your offices, habitual roles and status cues can make a relaxed and open conversation difficult.

- Will privacy be important for you or your informant? Although it might be impossible for anyone to eavesdrop in a crowded restaurant with a high noise level, some people feel inhibited by the mere presence of others.

Choosing an Approach

A variety of approaches can work for obtaining useful feedback. Here are several that have worked best for my clients, roughly in order of less to more formal.

Approach #1 The method of choice when you already have an easy relationship with someone is a conversation you initiate and in which you ask about a specific problem that your week of self-observation has brought into focus. It might sound something like this:

> Rod, I could use some help. At the staff meeting [during my presentation, etc.], I noticed that every time I came in with a comment, the conversation came to a standstill. There was a pause, and then a new topic was brought up. I think I may be doing something that's causing people to back off. Maybe I sound too positive, or maybe it's something else. My problem is I don't know what, or even if it's my imagination. What would really help me the most is your being as honest as you can. Don't worry about hurting my feelings. Whatever it is, I'm sure I can do something about it, and if I can't, at least it would help me to know what's happening.

The second version of this approach has a similar tone. You'll use it when you suspect that something is holding you back, but you're not sure what.

> Tom, I've been doing some deep thinking about myself and the job, and the fact that two promotions I thought I should

have had have gone to other people. I think there is something about the way I do things—something I do that I'm not really aware of—that's getting in the way. Since you've see me in action so much, I thought you might have noticed what's wrong or overheard other people say something about me that might be a clue to what might be holding me back.

Be sure to follow this initial statement with assurances that your feelings are not to be protected, that you're asking for information you believe you can use. This sets a positive note and relieves the other person of the necessity to be so diplomatic and gentle that the meaning is lost. Asking what others have *noticed* about you is useful, because it focuses them on what they've seen and helps them to describe your behavior rather than merely label you. Hearing that you're a "do it my way or else" kind of person, although somewhat informative, leaves you in the dark as to why you are seen that way. An observation that "there is sometimes an edge in your voice when you ask about problems," on the other hand, is far more useful, because it tells you what you need to change.

At times, people will be tempted to give you advice ("You need to listen more") rather than feedback ("You often cut people off before they are through talking"), so it's often helpful to candidly say, "I'm not asking for advice, just your impressions and particularly what you've noticed me doing." However, if advice is given, acknowledge it with thanks, then turn your friends' attention back to what they have seen, noticed, perceived, or felt about your behavior. Depending upon how wise or expert you believe them to be, you may indeed ask for advice later. Just remember that their ideas about what you need to do may fit their personalities and styles but not yours.

Approach #2   Sometimes it's worthwhile to try to get feedback from those to whom the idea of an open, feeling-level conversation seems inappropriate or even intimidating. In such cases, an approach that often works quite well is an adaptation of a method used in team-effectiveness training. This method works best if you can talk your boss into allowing you to use his or her name, because it provides a permissible setting for you to seek feedback, even in an organizational culture in which all are supposed to maintain an image of total self-confidence. Your opening will sound something like this:

> Jerry, the boss and I are trying to work up my training-and-development plan. He's given me some ideas, but I'd like to get as many impressions as I can of what I need to do to be more effective, particularly anything about my style that's getting in my way and that perhaps I'm not taking seriously enough. So, would you be willing to think about and jot down answers to a couple of questions and then pass them on to me next Friday when I come to call?
>
> There are only two questions, and it should only take you a few moments. Question one is, "If you and I were going to be team members for life, what three things would you like to see me do more of?" Question two is, "What would you like me to stop doing or do less of?" Please be as descriptive as you can, and don't worry about hurting my feelings. All I'm interested in is your perceptions and impressions.

In a second version, if you've asked several people for responses, you can ask that the slips of paper be dropped in a collection box, with or without signature. Anonymous information is better than none, but of course you can't follow up on it with specific questions. On the other hand, it may be more honest.

Approach #3   This approach works best after a performance review or in other circumstances in which you have been evaluated or criticized. For example, one of your coworkers may have burst out with, "You're not the only one who has ideas around here, you know!" Your goal will be to turn the criticism or complaint into a set of problem behaviors that you might choose to work on if they seem important enough. You accomplish this by posing a series of questions that help others be descriptive and specific. You can pick and choose among the following:

- I think I understand the situation, but could you tell me more about why it's a problem for you (for me)?

- What would you like me to do differently?

- How has my behavior affected you (others in the group, customers, and so forth)?

- Are there other things that you think would be helpful for me to work on?

- If I had to choose one or two of these problems, which should I work on first?

I particularly value this reaction to criticism because of its positive face. In addition, you show yourself to be strong and mature rather than troubled and defensive; thus you frustrate those who are trying to do you in, without in the least downplaying your part in the problem.

Prepare Yourself Psychologically

I have yet to meet someone who didn't find distasteful the idea of asking for feedback on potential problem behaviors; however, as often happens when events are dreaded, the confrontation is much less unpleasant in actuality than in anticipation. Nonetheless, since it's likely that you will contemplate these conversations with more than a little ambivalence, it's wise to take some specific steps to prevent your bold intentions from becoming sidetracked.

One obvious but still useful step is to tell someone else what you plan and why. Possibilities include a coworker, perhaps one that you intend to include in your list of interviewees, or someone at home. Give them permission to ask from time to time whether you have actually started your venture.

Jot down the list of the people with whom you expect to have conversations, and turn that list into an action plan. Indicate how and when you will be meeting with them, their phone or extension numbers (even the slight delay required to locate them in the phone directory can give your ambivalent self just the excuse it needs to put this whole nasty business off for a day when you're less busy). Then make an appointment with the first person on your list.

It's usually wise to start with someone with whom you have an ongoing, rather mellow relationship, even though your major concern is discovering why your boss casually asked if your spouse was still employed. Starting off in the most comfortable of uncomfortable circumstances will allow you time to refine your technique; and with each repetition, you will feel less tense. Your greater ease will then translate into less-biased responses from those whose perceptions you are trying to plumb.

Getting the Most from Your Conversations

You've made an appointment, chosen the most appropriate locale, set the stage by giving a positive face to your queries, and started off with the approach you deem the most promising. Your concern now is to obtain from these conversations the information you'll need to decide whether a commitment to change is in your best interest at the present time and, if so, what your targets should be. Here are some suggestions.

Encourage the Flow　Although you may have reassured your informant that your feelings won't be hurt, she will not be sure that you mean it until she tests you. To do that, she may start with a minor-league annoyance to see how you'll react. Regardless of how inaccurate or misinformed her comments about your behavior might be, avoid any explanations or corrections; they will be taken as defensive and a clear sign that you are not really prepared for any bad news. Instead, welcome what you hear with nodding head and appreciative noises—"That's great, just the kind of thing I hoped to hear." Always end with, "What else?" to encourage the flow to continue.

If your informant has spoken in generalities or simply labeled you ("Well, John, you know you're something of a complainer"), push her to be specific and to focus on what you do that leads her to see you as a member of that disagreeable tribe. Ask the usual kinds of descriptive questions: "Do you notice it at particular times?" "I don't mean to sound stupid, but could you tell me how you feel when I'm going on and on about how terrible our boss is?"

It's useful, from time to time, to check out your understanding by paraphrasing the gist of her comments. You'll not only ensure that you are not misinterpreting, but you'll let her know you're paying attention. Paraphrasing sounds something like this: "So, Mary, it looks to you as if I keep putting off telling my poor performers that they're screwing up. You think of me as someone who's always trying to be the nice guy, but not a very good manager. Have I got it right?"

Take Notes   Taking notes will serve several purposes: it demonstrates that you are indeed interested in what the other person is saying; it forces you to pay attention to what is being said, rather than to your inner shouts (or whimpers) of "I don't do that"; and it will also help you to avoid misremembering.

What If Your Informants Disagree?

It's not unusual to find several of your informants characterizing you differently enough to leave you feeling confused as to which version to believe. They may simply have observed you in different settings: while making public presentations, say, or exclusively in your role as a customer service rep. More commonly, the discrepancies will result from their personalities rather than yours. They interpret your behavior differently because they are using their own proclivities as benchmarks against which to judge the appropriateness of yours. To another highly analytic mind, your concern for accuracy and detail may be admirable, while to her more intuitive neighbor, "nitpicking bean counter" are the words that come to mind.

The best suggestions for making sense of these disparate views come from recent studies of interpersonal perception. Most important, they reaffirm the need to keep your informants focused on what you do and say, as well as how they feel about it. They are more likely to agree on the former, even when they disagree on the latter.

Give greater weight to your most competent informants—the best performers. They tend to be more observant and less biased toward seeing you in either a falsely positive or negative light.

Finally, *you* will need to be the final judge of the overall effects of your behavior, in full consideration of the reactions of those whose opinions are most important to you and with due respect for the power of your own defensiveness to coax you into discounting the downside of what you're hearing.

Watch Your Defensiveness

It's a good idea to assume that you feel more defensive than you think you do because it will alert you to watch out for inattention. It is emotionally tiring to listen to information that your behavior runs counter to that of the kind of person you want to be or think you are. If you find your attentiveness faltering, take a few seconds to review your notes, suggest a break for refreshments, or—if you have refreshments with you—take a moment to sip coffee or a soft drink. In those few seconds, pat yourself on the back for being courageous enough to do all this in the first place.

It's also possible that at some point you may feel overwhelmed and find yourself tearful, too anxious to sit still, or otherwise unable to sustain yourself in the interaction. In those circumstances, simply signal to your colleague that you'd like to call a time-out, during which you can regain your composure at least enough to talk about what has happened in a way that won't abort the conversation.

Several options can keep you in business by putting what's happened in perspective. Saying, "I'm getting just what I wanted, but that doesn't mean I like it," with as much of a smile as you can muster will help both of you continue. If that's not possible, suggest taking a break. It will enable you to get some privacy in which to acknowledge your own feelings and remind yourself that you've already made it through the worst part.

Reframe Your Doubts

It's a nice thought, but highly unlikely, that because you have bravely opened yourself to criticism, your inner defenses will simply fade away; they won't. Get set for insistent thoughts that "it's not really that bad" or "they're just too sensitive"—or even a flat "I just don't do that." Even when what you now hear echoes past comments from parents, spouses, or previous supervisors, you may try for a bit of false comfort by minimizing the extent to which your behavior was troublesome: "So I don't get all my reports in—does anybody ever read them, anyway?" Or, "Besides that"—your cagey defenses will point out—"it's your perceptions against theirs; there is no solid way to either confirm or deny those nasty allegations."

One way to counteract these all too normal defenses is to reframe the questions so that the focus is not on your goodness or badness—the areas your defenses are designed to protect—but on the more mundane question of how others react. Then, "They say I refuse to listen to my staff when they make suggestions" becomes "What is it that I do that makes my staff feel as if I am not paying attention to them?"

With this new focus, you can mentally reconstruct a recent interchange with a staff member: Did you interrupt before sentences were completed? Did you shuffle through the materials in your briefcase while others were still speaking? Were you thinking about your next move when you were supposed to be listening? Perhaps none of these behaviors interfered with your ability to pay attention, but that's not the point. For it doesn't take much imagination for you to see that those same behaviors might, indeed, seem self-centered and arrogant.

Too harsh a verdict? Is your self-esteem quaking? Not to worry. Remember that you have another line of defense—dumping the responsibility on someone or something else.

Counter Blaming Self and Blaming Others

True, blaming others is a handy device for staving off gloom when your best intentions don't produce the results you're after.

Are you too mature for that sort of childishness? Probably so, but no matter how confident you are in your ability to rise above such obvious immaturities, it's wise to expect that you'll respond to your collected lists of critical comments with suspicions that the failings of others or unfortunate circumstances are the real culprits. Less apparent but equally true, blaming yourself for being the kind of person you are, warts and all, can provide a quite serviceable basis for avoiding the whole troublesome business of sharpening up your presentation of yourself. If you're hopeless, why not just relax and enjoy being you? Remind yourself that such thoughts are normal and signify that the growth process you've started is moving along well. It *is* important, however, that you take some active steps to counter both kinds of blaming impulses, not by rejecting them out of hand—after all, they probably do have *some* foundation in fact—but by refocusing on that part of reality that the blaming helps you ignore.

This process works best if you record your thoughts in writing or enter them in your personal computer file. The task is simple. In the left column, note the blaming thoughts that have flitted through your mind. In the next column, jot down a brief statement that turns the blame into a developmental goal. Your list will look something like this:

- We have so much to do, I can't take the time to listen to all the comments my staff would like to make.

  So, how can I get decisions made without accruing resentment or resistance in my staff and having to closely supervise the implementation of all our work?

- I let poor performance go unchallenged because I've been afraid of conflict.

  How can a timid person go about setting clear standards and holding people to them?

- My bosses who have pushed me into this are not such great shakes themselves.

  Perhaps true, but if I want to get promoted, I still have to meet their perceptions of what a tough but not abrasive boss is like.

Whenever I've had to confront my own difficult behaviors, I've been impressed with how much negative energy I'd tied up in efforts to avoid facing the truth. Perhaps that is why I've always found this exercise not only valuable but relieving. For years, I had assumed that it was their lack of curiosity that led family and friends to signal nonverbally that they were less than enchanted by the informative little lecturettes that I foisted on them. The feedback that finally told me that, well-intentioned or not, my little displays of erudition often left them feeling either bored or one down was at first painful. But when I made myself refocus it as a target for change ("All I have to do is ask first whether they want my words of wisdom and keep my eye on their faces for signs that I've said too much"), the sudden lightness I felt told me that I had been unconsciously noticing that something was wrong, but resolutely denying it, for a long time.

In this connection, keep in mind that in general, men and women tend to react differently to feedback from others. Women, for example, seem to see negative feedback as descriptive of their native abilities rather than of how well they are applying specific skills. They are, therefore, often depressed by it. On the other hand, men, who in general tend to take a more competitive stance in work settings, tend to blame criticized behaviors on organizational pressures or the failings of others. The practical result is that, while women are more likely to think about feedback in terms of their own development, they often feel defeated in advance and settle for a lower level of performance than they otherwise might have obtained. Men, on the other hand, tend to maintain their self-confidence in the face of signs, both subtle and obvious, that some aspects of their performances are indeed holding them back. Both reactions provide sobering evidence of the power of blaming (oneself and others) to distort reality.

MAKING SENSE OF WHAT YOU'VE FOUND

At length, having weathered your information-collecting conversations and come to terms with your natural skepticism, you're ready to complete the process of making a realistic commitment to change. Still keeping a wary eye open for any last-minute defensive flurries your ego might whip up, review your painfully gathered assemblage of fact, perception, and misperception, and allow the major theme or themes to emerge.

Perhaps you are seen as so imposing that others hesitate to question, much less cross, you. The ugly words that tag along in this scenario are "pompous," "superior," and "closed minded." While your first thought might be, "Okay, from now on I won't be so imposing, pompous, superior, and closed minded," your second should certainly be, "Whatever all that means"—and it's a vitally important one if you are to convert a not very useful set of labels into behavioral targets toward which you can confidently aim. To find those targets, you must use your mélange of notes, the details you artfully coaxed out of your friends, your imagination, and perhaps even your mirror to generate specific answers to these three questions:

> *What* do I do and say—both verbally and nonverbally—that makes me seem imposing (indecisive, intimidating, superficial . . .) to others?
>
> *How* do I act to contribute to that impression?
>
> *What personal characteristics*—for example, my educational background or physical attributes—may add to the impact of my behavior?

It is your answers to these questions that become your targets for change.

Here is how each of these questions was addressed by Sally, who had been certified by all of her staff as "very imposing, pompous, closed minded, and superior." Notice that even at this stage she has some not unreasonable doubts.

"What do I do and say . . . ?"

- I guess I really don't listen past the first few sentences when I decide (too quickly?) either that I agree or don't agree.

- I start my replies (rebuttals?) with, "True, but . . ."

- I patiently explain why I'm right (thereby drowning out any improvements that others had in mind).

- I delegate a job and then tell the person how to do it. I have evidently (did I or didn't I?) often taken over a project when the person assigned ran into a problem.

"How do I act . . . ?"

- My voice gets harder (don't quite know what that means yet—ask my husband) when I get in an argument.

- I sometimes slam the table when someone keeps coming at me.

- My face evidently turns red when I'm getting angry, even though my voice doesn't get louder.

- I glare (stare?) a lot.

"What personal characteristics . . . ?"

- My Harvard degree and MBA? Have I used them to overwhelm opposition? Better check it out. The problem is that I am smarter and more knowledgeable than everyone else, except maybe Sheri. Why is that a problem?

- I dress well. I won't change this.

You can see from Sally's notes that, as well as helping you identify target behaviors, describing yourself from the perspective of how you appear to others also stimulates useful dialogue with yourself and pinpoints areas in which you may need to do additional fact finding.

If you've already attempted to modify some of the target behaviors that show up on your list, you may feel angry—at both yourself and your informants—and discouraged that your prior efforts haven't worked. Take heart! Studies of how people deal with self-destructive behaviors in everyday life show that those who have successfully modified even the most intractable behaviors have often had a number of aborted or otherwise unsuccessful tries. The best motto to keep in mind when the memory of past unsuccessful efforts tempts you to relegate your notes to a file drawer or the wastebasket is that of therapists Richard Bandler and John Grinder: "There are no failures, only feedback." For unless everything we know about how to deal with painful situations is wrong, knowing that you've made the effort to collect information and that you have a plan for using it—that you're in control—should help your poor struggling ego to survive the assault. After all, you've already done the hardest part. You've looked into the mirror and identified just what needs modifying. Now, reminding yourself that even small changes can bring large benefits, you're ready to decide what you're going to do differently and how and when you are going to do it—the very subjects of Chapter 3.

3

Planning How,
When, and Where
to Start Your
Program

With the toughest steps—identifying troublesome behaviors and setting targets for change—behind you and the decision to do something about them pushing you to get it over with, you may feel ready to get right to work. Perhaps your problem behavior seems simplistically easy to manage—just listen more and let up on the smart remarks, maybe. So taking the time to carefully think through what you're going to do and then turning those thoughts into a written plan of action may seem complicating and unnecessary. But there are good reasons for having a plan before you move into action, and even better reasons why it's unwise to start without one, as newly hired brokerage analyst Doug Keely discovered.

Doug had been on the job for four months. He was bright, confident, and ambitious, just what you'd expect from a young Wharton MBA. But this late spring afternoon, he was slouched down in his junior-executive chair, still smarting from the patient, somewhat patronizing lecture he had just been handed by his supervisor. Still, he was determined that he wasn't going to let a bruised ego prevent him from achieving the success he knew his ability entitled him to.

"All right," he thought, "so I sounded too flip and casual to some of my brokerage customers. Coming across as substantial and serious shouldn't be much of a problem for a solid citizen like me."

He listened in on his older associates' phone conversations and dreamed up an image of a more mature Doug who projected seriousness of intent and weighty wisdom. For the next few weeks, he was the epitome of Doug Keely, straight-arrow stockbroker.

A month later the shocker came. "I'm sorry, Doug," his boss said, "but I don't think that this is the game for you. I've had two of your accounts call me asking for a new analyst, and this morning's mail brought a rollover request to move a sizable retirement account to another brokerage house. I had hopes that our little talk a while ago would straighten you out, but it seems to have made things worse."

"But what do they say I was doing wrong?" Doug wailed. "You said be more businesslike, so I sat up straight in my chair, stopped the chitchat, and became serious."

"Well, that explains the complaints that you were negative, distant, and uninvolved. I suppose that could be the real problem—maybe you just don't care about your customers."

If you are thinking to yourself, "Wait a minute, Doug simply started off solving the wrong problem—he just needed better feedback, not a plan," you are partly right. If he had followed up his boss's original lecture with some additional assessment, he might have seen that his casual demeanor had seemed insincere—as if he were taking his customers' problems lightly—rather than informal. Yet even in retrospect, his mistake was an easy one to make.

I started this chapter with Doug Keely's example because I've witnessed too many instances of initially enthusiastic efforts at behavior remodeling that faltered because the remodelers initially headed off target. In their eagerness, they had not thought long enough about which specific behavioral changes might actually alter others' perceptions of them. And like Doug, they had given even less consideration to the way they would monitor how well they were doing, an essential step that might have prompted the corrective maneuvers needed to keep Doug on track. So one of the best reasons for taking the time to plan is that it tests the accuracy of your initial assessment by forcing you to translate information and interpretations into action steps. But there are even more reasons for planning before you act.

Before you can plan, you must first sort out the pieces of your puzzle, asking yourself: How does that troublesome behavior work for me? Can I keep some of those satisfactions without dragging along the unintended liabilities that get in my way? Are there certain people or situations that bring on the behavior that I'm trying to modify? Are there similar situations in which I don't display the troublesome behavior? The answers to these and similar questions will shape how you will go about doing things differently.

Then, too, a plan will help you make the best use of your efforts. You'll chose the best times to try out new behavior; you'll work on changes that are neither too difficult nor inconsequential; and most important, by covering all the important bases, you'll provide yourself with a solid foundation for success.

Changing behaviors that have become habitual is usually an uncomfortable and unnatural undertaking. Whether you are changing your grip on a tennis racket or learning to stay silent when you feel your temper simmering, you might as well expect a protesting inner groan and an impulse to return to what feels right. A plan, replete with steps to be followed, cautionary alerts, and sketchy scripts for filling embarrassed silences, will help you stay the course long enough to see that you can indeed manage the weakness without losing the strength.

Finally, there is good evidence that commitments that are written down gain strength, especially when they are discussed with another person. Converting thoughts to written symbols not only makes them concrete but it becomes your first action step, increasing the likelihood that tasks will be promoted from "should do it" to "will do it." It also may lessen any onus you might feel to acknowledge that you may not be entirely perfect. Or maybe it's as uncomplicated as converting a feeling-laden experience into just another task to be undertaken, another problem to be solved. Whichever of these reasons seem persuasive to you, think your way through a plan of action and jot down the essence of it. It will help.

On the other hand, too much writing down can be a problem too. Travis, that careful administrator from Section I, ended up with four pages of neatly written planning notes that answered every conceivable eventuality, including lists of suggested words and phrases appropriately columned with the situations in which they would be most useful. The plan was so bulky that it was never available when he needed it. So keep your plan simple, keep it skeletal, and keep it short enough to fit onto something that you can slip into your calendar, wallet, or anything else that is with you during those moments when you are most likely to trip yourself up. To get to that succinct action plan, you'll need to briefly answer these questions:

- What have you done differently in those situations in which you haven't been difficult?

- What situations lure you into difficult behavior?

- What will you do or not do differently?

- How, when, and where will you start?

- How will you know you've made progress?

The answers to these questions will constitute your action plan.

WHAT HAVE YOU DONE DIFFERENTLY IN THOSE SITUATIONS IN WHICH YOU HAVEN'T BEEN DIFFICULT?

No one is always difficult. It's true that the difficult behavior you're trying to manage is a part of that mix of verbal and non-verbal behaviors, temperaments, motivations, and strategies that make up what we call personality. Still, you don't behave

that way all the time. More often than not, you are calm and attentive, do listen to others, and don't leave others feeling derogated.

Whatever behavioral themes emerged from your data gather-
ing, there will always have been times when you were not super-
cilious, imposing, or arrogant, nor were you perceived that way.
Return in memory to those exceptional times. How was the situation different from those that elicited your problem behavior?
Were there differences in the way you felt about the behavior of
others? Were you feeling pleased about an accomplishment, less
tense about the pressures at work?

Often the differences will seem slight—the same words spoken but with a less demanding tone, for example. By thinking
through those felicitous occasions, you can often find clues that
will point you toward ways of behaving that are already in your
repertoire. You'll need only to polish them up and learn to cue
them into action as substitutes for their difficult behavioral
cousins.

WHAT SITUATIONS LURE YOU INTO DIFFICULT BEHAVIOR

Having identified the circumstances that evoke your most effective behavior, you'll find it equally useful, if less comforting, to
get a fix on the situations that set you up to be difficult. If you
can identify just when you're most likely to slip, you can be
watchful, ready to hold back an impulse to do or say something
you know you'll later regret.

As you might expect, these hazardous places all are connected
with a fundamental human need to defend yourself from a real
or fancied assault on your psychological vitals.

In general, difficult behaviors are most likely to be evoked under these conditions: when you feel both threatened and under
pressure to act; when you feel demeaned or humiliated; when
you feel an overload of stress; when you feel low; and when you
are in physical settings that trigger remembrances of any of these
feelings. As you mull over this list of situations and the amplifi-
cations below, search both your memory and your feedback
notes for clues that some or all have consistently accompanied
the behaviors you've targeted.

Feeling Defensive and Pressured to Act

The trouble is, like all human beings, you've evolved as a creature with a too efficient mechanism for defense. In this context, of course, you're not defending against physical danger, but against attacks—real or fancied—on your image of the person you'd like to be, or at least the person you would like others to believe you to be. In everyday life, most of us have to cope with a rather steady barrage of blows to our sense of self-worth, often delivered by people who have something else entirely in mind. We may be sitting at our desks reviewing a report when we hear Tom, an office mate whom we've always thought of as a particular friend, inviting fellow worker Joanne to lunch. The invitation is not extended to us. Our vulnerable self wonders, "Why Joanne and not me?"

Then there are those words and actions that leave us feeling one down, that is, derogated, demeaned, or found wanting in relation to someone whose regard we care about. We proudly present to our respected colleague a key position paper into which we've put our creative souls, wanting a word of praise, perhaps even admiration. Instead, our reward is a bare glance, a mumbled "Yes, this will do," and an empty feeling as we watch him drop our masterpiece onto an already overflowing pending basket. If we take our respected colleague's dismissal as impugning our status or competence, and react as most of us would, we will no longer try for equal footing. Instead, we will strive somehow to get one up on *him;* never mind that it will likely cost *us* in reputation or personal effectiveness.

For example, Doug Keeley's ill-concealed disinterest when his boss lectured him did, indeed, boost him from one down ("I'm being treated like an ignoramus; doesn't he know I've already studied this stuff?") to one up ("This guy is boring, and I'll oh-so-cleverly show him I think so"). But it also jump-started his boss's need to regain his proper one-up position by showing Doug who was really in charge. A more insightful Doug might have recognized that his impulse to show up his boss was prompted by his feeling demeaned, and been able to summon up a more productive response, neither striving for one up nor accepting one down ("I think I'm up on puts and calls, Boss, but could you go over the policy on which customers we notify of hot stock offerings?").

Did Doug's boss, or Tom, or the respected colleague intend harm? Probably not consciously, although in fact, Tom may have meant to exclude us because we talk too much, and the respected colleague may be so ego driven that he truly doesn't see us as important enough for his full attention. Either way, the result will be an anguished sense of hurt, as if some vital part has been damaged. Beneath the hurt, of course, is fear—fear that someone has sabotaged the fulfillment of our deepest motivations. To be sure, someone else in exactly the same circumstances may have been unmoved by either slight. While all human beings do share a common body of wants and needs, they are moved by them to quite varying degrees.

For some, being in charge is vital, and it is when they see others whittling away at their authority that they feel most threatened. Others may have little need to be in charge, but they want to be liked, accepted, or acknowledged by others. Still others of us care little about control or lovability but need to constantly feel competent and challenged—if they need anything from their fellow human beings it's that those whose opinions they respect recognize the quality and importance of their achievements.

By the time they're adults, most people have acquired at least enough insulation over their most vulnerable motivational areas to avoid perpetual panic about being cut down, but some remain highly sensitive to attack. As you might expect, in another one of those nice and nasty human ironies, it is the high powered and highly motivated who are most easily and quickly threatened by a hint that their interpersonal skills are wanting. If you are one of those individuals, keep in mind that when you are under pressure to act—and just at that moment you're feeling hurt, unappreciated, or challenged—you are particularly liable to engage in your favorite defensive measures.

We each have our own favorites. Yours may be angry yelling; mine may be stubborn argument or withdrawal; someone else's may simply be self-blaming and going along with what everyone else wants to do. Still others may choose to play the clown. Whatever your preference in defensive tactics, you learned them very early in life, because they worked well enough to get you out of interactional pickles. If tears and "I'm sorry's" brought forgiveness and parental hugs as a child, giving in and going along in the face of conflict and pressure is likely to be your first line of defense as an adult.

Certainly the most basic law of learning is "If it works, use it"—especially if it continues to work; and a flaring temper can usually be counted on to immobilze the opposition just as well as your temper tantrums did as a kid. The difference is that in childhood it was only the short-term result—saving your skin—that counted. Now you have to concern yourself with longer-term effects, most of which are negative, which is exactly why you started this program.

Three criteria can help you determine whether your difficult behavior is one of these protective maneuvers carried over from your early days:

- Does the tone of your words and actions have a disjointed quality (they don't fit well with the mood of what was happening just before your outburst, tears, withdrawal, or joking around)?

   Because your defensive behavior is not tied to the substance of a discussion but to a suspected attack on your always vulnerable psyche, your emotional line of defense may be engaged suddenly, startling both yourself and others. For example, during a spirited discussion about a new product design, you might find yourself saying, "Well, I guess if that's what you folks want to do, I'll go along." The precipitating event was not a cogent argument against your favorite design, but a barely overheard scrap of off-scene conversation that coupled your name—well, it might have been your name—with a dismissive snigger.

   In sum, don't dismiss the power of that deadly combination: personal threat plus the pressure to act. In fact, it is this "cocktail" that is so frequently lethal in barrooms and on the street.

- Does your attacking, evasive, or withdrawing behavior feel as if it's jerked out of you rather than deliberately displayed? Accumulating evidence does suggest that there may

be several thinking and perceptual mechanisms in opera-
tion at the same time. The largest, and certainly the most
recently evolved, contains your memories and a collection
of intuitive and learned strategies for dealing with the
world that you use in planning and problem solving. But
there is also another, far more basic perceptual apparatus,
lurking just below the level of awareness, concerned solely
with primitive assessment.

The information stored in the much larger and higher-
level data bank is accessed as you acquire information on
how best to handle whatever is confronting you. Responses
from the other level, however, are accessed almost instanta-
neously and are subject only to a primitive feeling test: "It's
dangerous" or "It's not dangerous." By the time your reasonable, rational mind becomes aware of what's happening, that primitive pre-mind has already shoved you into a
shouted attack or silent submission—the modern-day
equivalents of thrusting a spear or playing dead—to foil
whatever vague growling shape has leaped from the branch
above. From this perspective, it makes sense that your more
dramatic difficult behaviors seem to happen to you at the
same instant that they have descended on your targets.

- When the episode is finished, do you feel confused and un-
certain as to why you behaved as you did? Do you sometimes apologize later for having behaved that way? Because
ancestral defensive maneuvers are usually at odds with the
rules for proper conduct that you may have been taught as
a child, it would be surprising if, after the fact, you didn't
wonder guiltily, "Why did I behave that way?" Most social-
conduct rules are, in truth, designed to inhibit impulses to
behave naturally. The control doesn't always hold, however, because the impulses are strong *and* because the expressive release of feelings, accompanied by your
occasional successes at tantrum domination, are highly reinforcing.

Although important, attacks on your psychological vitals are
not the only situational elements that can evoke your repertoire

of difficult behaviors. You own mood swings, stress overload, and even the physical settings in which your troublesome behavior erupts are well worth considering in drawing up your "when and where I need to be alert" list.

Moodiness

Some people are subject to sizable mood swings. When their moods are up, they weather sizable storms with equanimity. When their moods are down, however, comparatively minor or accidental mishaps can provoke withdrawal or angry attack.

Keep in mind that not all moodiness is internally generated. If your work has a cyclical turn to it—that is, you have complex reports due every first of the month or a weekly editorial to get out, or the monthly sales figures are published every third Thursday—you may become more irritable as those trying times draw near. The point is, whatever the cause of your moodiness, be particularly ready to manage your behavior. Here's how Fred Barker, owner of a small manufacturing business, put it:

> "You know, I didn't really think of my downtimes as black moods until I overheard my secretary telling someone on the telephone that the hardest thing about working with her boss was that one week he was Saint George and the next week he was the dragon. Now, when I'm feeling grumpy—that's the way I used to excuse it, 'just being a little grumpy'—I try to keep away from people as much as I can. When I can't avoid it, like in a meeting, I just keep thinking to myself, 'Bite your tongue. It's not them, it's you.'"

Stress Overload

An overly full measure of personal stress tends to push most people to mentally hunker down. That is, they work almost exclusively on those daily tasks they can control with their basic and habitual strategies and skills. It's useful to keep that in mind when, as the Red Queen put it in *Through the Looking Glass,* you feel the need to "run faster just to stay in place" or, even more important, when the symptoms of overloading stress—sleep or digestive disturbances, bouts of unusual forgetfulness, an increase in muscle tension in the back, legs, or neck—warn you that your body has settled into a sustained emergency mode. That is just when your strengths are most likely to become liabilities and you slide back into stubbornly held dogmas, endless equivocations, or a "do it and shut up" mode. It may also be a time for a serious reflection on the need to pull back to a more deliberate pace and to reset your priorities.

Physical Settings

Physical settings, their smells, sights, sounds, and other sensations, can evoke deep memories of past defeats and disasters. I can still recall the angry, resistant feelings that overwhelmed me when, to begin my program of doctoral studies, I entered the small office of my major professor. Although I was in my forties and an active and successful professional person, his oak desk strewn with student papers and the pair of straight-backed oak chairs sitting primly by the desk took me back to the school principal's office, where I had felt shamed and ridiculed when I was a young boy. Try as I might over the next three years, I continued to feel on edge in that setting, and I still regret my inability to make full use of the counsel of a very wise and supportive mentor.

Look for ways to avoid key interactions, especially if they've been troublesome in the past, in those places most likely to elicit the behaviors you wish to avoid. For example, if you are an expert know-it-all, like Sally, you may want to conduct your important meetings outside your own office, if that temple of authority nudges you toward pompous impatience with the incompetence of others.

It's not that difficult behavior is always so hard to manage; in fact, the action steps you'll settle on may seem almost anticlimactically simple. Often far more elusive, however, is getting a fix on just how your behavior should change.

WHAT WILL YOU DO OR NOT DO DIFFERENTLY?

Start by reviewing your feedback notes, then list the target behaviors you've decided to focus on; they tell you what you need to stop doing, do less of, or do more of. Do you need to curb some aspects of your behavior? Do you need to learn some new techniques and skills or fill in knowledge gaps? Perhaps all you need is to buttress your own weak areas by working closely with a partner who is strong just where you are not. Or perhaps you need to employ some combination of all of these.

Identify Substitute Behaviors

Separately consider each of your targets. What words and actions would serve as workable substitutes for your problem behaviors in the settings in which you most frequently find yourself? To break a habitual response or block an impulse to action, you need to have handy counteracting behaviors, socially acceptable alternatives for the moves your mind and body are aching to make. You'll use these substitute behaviors when your difficult behavior has escaped your best intentions to contain it. For example, just as you find yourself once again saying yes when you should be saying no, you can avoid the worst effects of having gone along with a bad idea with a recovery ploy like, "That is, I think it might be okay, but I need to think it through—I'll get back to you in ten minutes."

Substitute behaviors work best when they're formulary, that is, when they have been so thoroughly scripted and well rehearsed that you can get them out even in moments of anger, confusion, or panic. So in devising your own, you'll want to stay consonant with your interpersonal style and your physical attributes.

Fits Your Style   Your object in behavior management is not to become a different person, merely a less heavily baggaged one. So your substitute behaviors ought to fit your basic motivations and ways of looking at things. If you are an aggressive person, motivated to get into action quickly and drive forcefully toward your objectives, your method for handling disagreements can't smack of passivity or surrender. Sure, a passive response would avert feeding your intimidator image, but at the cost of unnecessarily frustrating you and baffling everyone else.

A better choice would be a phrase that leaves you in charge but uses your control to convert your role from one of telling to one of listening. For instance, one of the most empowering team leaders I've known, a person with a huge need to be dominant, started off staff meetings by announcing, "I want all points of view expressed. They *will* be paid attention, they *will* be acknowledged. All of the above includes me, and I expect to be called on it if I violate these rules." Was he autocratic? Yes. Was the nature of the discussion imposed on the group? Yes. But his direction was aimed at making it open and interactive, and his behavior demonstrated that his intention was to stop intimidating where it counted. It worked well.

However, your style is only partially defined by what you say and intentionally do; everything else about you communicates nonverbally, and much of what is communicated is only partially under your control.

Nonverbal Communication Here are some characteristics of nonverbal communication to consider as you formulate the counteracting moves that you will substitute for your target behaviors:

- Many facial expressions are hardwired to perceptions of danger or pleasure and, therefore, are to some extent irrepressible; they tend to leak out when feelings or motivations are high. Because of the extreme effort it takes to override the hardwiring, simply suppressing the expression of strong emotions can make you look wooden, cold, or secretive.

- Your facial expressions are less accessible to you than to others. That's one reason why they see and hear you differently than you see yourself. You say (and believe it when you say it): "I'm not accusing anybody. I'm just trying to find out what happened." They see your eyes narrowed, your face red, your body leaning forward in an attack position.

- Nonverbal behavior is seldom talked about directly. Conversations precipitated by it focus on feelings inferred by others from it, not on the behavior itself. For example, upon seeing you frowning with a tense expression around your eyes, your partner says, "You look worried." Your reply, "No, I'm not worried," closes off the communication. Therefore, your partner's incorrect inferences about the meaning of those facial expressions (that you were really mad) are never clarified.

Thus far, I've not provided a very promising picture. What's the point of working hard to say and do things differently, if your face and body posture give away your real feelings? If nonverbal behavior is so intractable and trying to hide it may simply trade one problem for another, should you attempt to do anything at all with it?

I believe the best answer is yes within some limits; these limits are your abilities as an actor and your willingness to tamper with and practice your presentation skills (more about this in the next chapter). People can learn—and almost universally have learned—to successfully portray emotions different from those they actually feel, although the portrayal is usually less intense than the real thing.

The most important point is, don't try to do too much. Select one or two of the looks or gestures that may be adding to the negative impact of the behavior you're trying to correct, and practice subtly altering them. Do you frown when you're merely concentrating and unknowingly evoke angry or defensive reactions? Do you nod your head "yes" when you're thinking "no"? Does your index finger jab the air for emphasis, violating your listener's personal space? When listening, do you gaze out of the window, rather than at the speaker? These and similar nonverbal foibles have been successfully countered by adopting substitute behaviors that interdicted or repaired the damage. As always, your goal will be to find new gestures that reflect your true feelings, but without the negative spin that unintentionally accompanied the old.

It's wise to expect that when you feel stressed or pressured or are concentrating intently, some of your old behaviors may leak through. Therefore, you'll need to invent substitute behaviors that can do repair duty when you suddenly realize you've slipped. For example, you might acknowledge the thoughts or feelings that prompt your drumming fingers and impatient wriggling, but factor out the attacking or defensive aspects: "Do I look upset? It's just that I'm worried about the deadline and I'm wondering if this small talk is a help or hindrance to getting the job done." The first part of that phrase constitutes the substitute behavior, words that you've carefully composed and practiced as an automatic response to the sight of your drumming fingers.

Fits Your Physical Attributes   Hank Kahn, who headed his own insurance agency, was six feet, four inches tall and weighed 225 pounds. A former professional hockey player, he moved with imposing grace, stated his opinions forcefully, and complained that he was surrounded by yes-people. It turned out that one major reason for this was his habit of starting staff meeting discussions with, "We should . . ." Since he often accompanied these seeming dictates with an openhanded sideways swipe over the tabletop (left over from his hockey days?), his staff assumed that he had already made the decision without the benefit of any input from them. Having received their marching orders, they carefully refrained from disputing the wisdom of those decisions, although often they privately believed them to be stupid and impossible to implement, a judgment with which a puzzled Hank usually concurred.

Believing that this "minor communications problem" would be easy to fix, Hank worked out a set of substitute behaviors—he would take a backseat in the discussion process and try "What I think is . . ." instead of his old "We should . . ."

A month later, he complained: "Dr. Bramson, there is no way that I can look meek and mild. I've tried slumping in the chair, but my back, which is banged up anyway, won't take it. I've folded my hands in my lap, but when I get excited, I thump the table from underneath, making everyone think I'm nuts. How do I get them to believe that I really want them to speak up? Changing what I say doesn't seem to be enough."

"So," I summed up, "it looks like no matter what your words

say, your position as boss and your general mass say, 'Listen up.' Sounds like your best alternative is to intimidate them into disagreeing with you. How can you do that?"

Here is what Hank came up with:

- At least at the beginning, dress down during staff meetings (take off jacket, loosen tie).

- Stand up when I bring up an issue to be discussed, and then sit down as soon as the discussion starts.

- Order them to find fault with my ideas and make that a performance-evaluation standard.

- Privately talk to my senior sales agent about what I'm trying to do, and coach her on how to argue with me, even when I get excited.

Each of these substitute steps worked well, except for the first one. Shirtsleeves and loosened tie made Hank look *more* imposing, rather than less. The basic point once again is not to try to seem passive and receptive if your size, shape, and general demeanor communicate power and aggressiveness, and conversely, don't set yourself up to bark out commands if your voice is high and squeaky.

The general flavor of workable substitute behaviors is captured in these examples drawn from my case notes (you'll find more examples of substitute behaviors in Chapters 6 to 9):

- As a substitute for "Just do it!" say, "Wait a minute, could you tell me again what you want to do (were trying to say)?"

- Used by a customer services representative who looked angry when thinking: "Am I frowning? It's because I'm trying to decide."

- Used as a repairing step by a supervisor with a talent for biting sarcasm who could not or would not give it up: "That was sarcasm—I was just trying to make a point."

- As a substitute for giving in and going along: "Sorry, Jan, but the policy is 'no raises right now' . . . Well, I suppose we could make an except— No. It's just not possible."

Two questions that we briefly touched upon elsewhere may have resurfaced for you: can you believably behave in ways that are not consistent with your feelings and natural impulses and, even if you could, is it ethical to do so?

Are Substitute Behaviors Ethical?

There is ample evidence that people can and do spend much of their work lives behaving as they believe others want and expect them to, and they generally do a credible job of performing. There is also consistent evidence that with a good script, ample feedback, and sufficient rehearsal, you can get so proficient at performing in those new roles that you will often be hard pressed to distinguish the part you play in them from your natural self. For example, if you are basically a shy person but you have developed yourself into an effective public speaker, you will have discovered that you can pretend to be confident and at ease, and at times it will even feel as if you were having fun.

For me, the ethical question is one of intentions. Am I substituting a learned behavior for my natural response in order to take advantage of you? If so, then I am indeed behaving unethically. If, on the other hand, I am using that substitute behavior to enhance my value to you as well as myself, then I am not only behaving ethically but intelligently as well. For example, let's say I find that my habit of gazing out of the window while thinking hard communicates to my clients that I am not paying attention. If I intend that they think me inattentive, then I should stick with my window gazing. But if I want them to know that I am attentive, then it behooves me to substitute looking at their eyes, mouths, or noses (they won't know the difference). Alternatively, I could explain to them that my window gazing indicates I'm concentrating hard on what they're saying. Both are ways of purposefully coping with my difficult behavior. If I'm not sure whether I will always remember to gaze at them rather than a dusty windowpane, I ought to include both substitute behaviors in my coping plan.

DEVELOPMENTAL PLANNING IN ACTION

Doug Keely was lucky enough to be given a second chance and, determined to use the opportunity well, he generated these planning notes.

What I learned from the feedback:

- The two customers that complained most were retired or close to retired, and I'm not up on the type of income-producing investments they were interested in.

- I need to admit to myself that I felt so busy that I haven't boned up on their investment histories.

- Millie, my cubicle neighbor, mentioned that my answers to customers' questions seemed to show a lot of latitude ("Would utility stocks be a good investment?" "Well, it all depends on how the economy is going."). When I asked her if she was politely telling me that I BS a lot when I don't know the answer, she said, "That too." Very funny, but did she mean more?

- My boss, Charlie, said that when I'm talking to him, I'm often looking out the window, that when I smile while he's instructing me about something (usually something I already know about), I have a smart-ass look about me (need to check that out in the mirror).

What personal characteristics . . . ?

- I'm younger than all of my customers (at least I look younger to me).

What have I done differently those times when things have gone well?

- I had a really good session with Joe Glover. He's younger; his goal is growth, not income; and I got him fervently interested in a plan to mix and match his small company stocks with metals and offshore companies. These are areas in which I've been interested myself and in which I've done a lot of reading. Conclusion: get and stay knowledgeable, dummy!

What lures me into being difficult?

- People who are important to me, who are older or have authority, seem to make me want to act cool.

- When I feel I'm being talked down to, ditto, maybe with an edge.

- When the conversation gets to something I'm supposed to be expert in but I'm not, I seem to have trouble saying, "I don't know, but I'll find out."

What do I need to do or not do? (My targets!!!)

- I need to give them confidence that although I'm young, I know what I'm doing—by increasing my knowledge base re needs of present customers, that is, read up more about income-producing investments.

- When asked, give my best judgment rather than evading the question with a platitude (do I really do that?). If I catch myself in a platitude, I'll finish my sentence and then say, "But in your case, I think that . . ." and then give my best judgment.

- I need to behave so that customers will know that I'm interested in them:

  —no generalities to show off my book learning
  —listen and think about what they're saying
  —make sure to study customer files even if I have to stay late, and especially with older customers
  —start off each customer meeting by asking a lot of questions to help me get focused (and to show them that I'm interested)

- Stop turning people off by sounding (and looking) arrogant. Be alert to what sets me up for this.

  —When I'm with customers, watch out for thoughts that they must be dumb or too ancient to matter. When I catch myself having those thoughts, sit forward in the chair, pull out the funds book, and start looking through it as if I've just thought of something.

Having identified—preferably in spare and easily readable language—the most important changes you need to make, you're ready to decide how, when, and where you'll start.

HOW, WHEN AND WHERE WILL YOU START?

The most important characteristic that distinguishes those who consistently succeed in just about any enterprise from those who do not is the level of difficulty of the goals that they set for themselves. The repeated failures of generally unsuccessful people stem from goals either so easy that they confirm the triviality of the effort or so ambitious that they can't be attained with available resources. In contrast, the consistently successful select moderate goals for themselves, just tough enough that achieving them adds to their store of personal efficacy, but modest enough to be attained even when luck is bad. Since corralling troublesome behaviors is hardly ever an easy task, it's worthwhile to take these lessons to heart by initially planning to tackle no more than two of your target areas. Also, take your first crack at them under circumstances that are most likely to lead to a feeling of mastery. For example, the "how, when and where" portion of Doug Keely's plan looked like this:

- Start with customers in the thirty-to-forty-five-year-old age range—less intimidating to me (two coming up in the next week).

- Try to reserve the small conference room instead of meeting with them in my cubicle.

- What I'll do and say:

  —get them to talk about their goals; listen; make notes
  —stop myself from interrupting or, if too late, say, "Please finish what you were going to say."
  —practice new, nonarrogant smile in front of the mirror, starting tonight

- Develop a good list of income and balanced funds; brief myself on a dozen sound munis and/or corporate bond possibilities.

Viewed against the number and complexity of his daunting list of target behaviors, Doug's action plan seems rather puny. Wasn't he being too easy on himself?

Certainly, if his total plan was limited to boning up on the finer points of bond investments, that would, while useful, make little progress against the more personal aspects of his problem behavior. And if he is to fully benefit from his efforts, they will have to focus on a wider variety of customers, especially senior citizens of high status and grim visage. It's even true that the conference room will not often be available to him and he'll need to learn how to maintain his dignity in a cubicle. Yet my sense was that he would find in these initial steps a crucial boost to his belief that it is indeed possible to manage those subtle, irritating behaviors that led him to this effort in the first place.

There are other reasons for starting slow. For one thing, initial changes that are too encompassing, especially if they are successful, can induce paradoxical efforts on the part of friends, even those who wanted you to shape up, to subtly bring you back to "normal" ("You're so serious now, Doug. What are you trying to do, kiss up to the brass and get to be vice president?").

Second, moderate behavioral targets will make it easier to make judgments about how much change is really needed, since much of the time a little less, or a little less often, will make the difference. As this whole enterprise is likely to be far from your favorite occupation, it makes sense to go step by step and gradually make more refined estimates of your progress.

There is a third, more subtle, reason for limiting your initial efforts. Although most difficult behaviors are your reasonable responses to the barriers and brambles of life, difficult only because of their unintended effects, some problem behaviors may be the result of more deeply buried emotional blips. Let's say, for instance, that Doug Keely's occasional episodes of arrogance were symptoms of a still-fermenting rebellion against his parents. Some psychotherapists (those who specialize in long-term therapy, naturally) make the point that if that sort of deeper conflict isn't addressed, it will continue to intrude. While Doug might successfully do away with his insolent smile, they suggest, his hidden "up yours" impulses would emerge elsewhere.

One way to hedge your bets is to tackle your behavior change incrementally over a longer period of time. You will then have breathing spaces in which to evaluate whether, having taken out of one set of symptoms, you have substituted another. If your answer is "yes" or "perhaps," conversations with a counselor before venturing further may indeed be wise. (We'll consider this question more carefully in Chapter 10.)

How Will You Know You've Made Progress?

Since possibilities for change are unlimited, your plan should have a few mileposts to tell you when you've reached a reasonable stopping place. Avoid general statements such as, "My customers will know I'm sincere." Instead, describe, with as much specificity as possible, just what circumstances will mark that blessed state; for example, "No more than one customer of mine over any six-month period will ask to be transferred to another investment counselor."

Some other examples are:

"I'll respond to eighty percent of my phone messages, at least four days out of five."

"Customers with complaints will end by thanking me instead of getting defensive."

"My boss will note that I've been listening more."

"My temper won't get out of hand for two weeks in a row."

"The committee members who were out for my scalp will have stopped talking about me."

Whom Can You Enlist to Help or Support You?

It is helpful, although not essential, to have a support person on call who can provide you with an empathic ear or be a sounding board—always helpful for keeping a balanced perspective—during those moments of doubt that accompany any difficult task. Unfortunately, there is a caveat—such a person can be helpful if she has the right qualities, but can, if wrongly chosen, interfere with, even derail, your efforts. So it's worth taking the time to match your support candidates against a few general criteria and then to keep the person who best fits these criteria clearly in mind.

If you don't, when your first efforts have brought you either elation or discouragement, you may be tempted to seek comfort or approbation from whoever is most conveniently around. If that person turns out to be, for example, one of those sweet people who confuse sympathy with support or a cynic who is sure that no one can change, the potential for learning much from your initial experiences will be lost, and you may even accede to your own impulses to bail out of your program.

In the next chapter, we'll examine ways you can best use your support person as a coach and how you can involve both your boss—and subordinates, if you have them—in providing encouragement and added feedback, both of which can increase the pace of your learning. With that in mind, plan on using these criteria when deciding whom among your friends, family, or coworkers to enlist as your source of support:

- You respect their competence, even though their abilities and experience may lie in areas different from your own.

- You have confidence that they will keep your conversations confidential if you make it clear that this is what you expect.

- They will be direct and candid with you when you've made it clear that this is what you want.

- They listen reasonably well; that is, they seldom cut you off midsentence, override your statements with their own advice, or otherwise fill most of the available conversational space.

- They don't appear to be overly judgmental; in other words, their part of the conversation isn't overloaded with "you should's," "you ought to have's," and similar prescriptive phrases. They don't substitute general formulas for living— "Never let anyone get the best of you"—for specific suggestions on how you might have handled a situation about which you've reported.

- A sense of humor is always an asset.

- When choosing between several candidates, search for someone who counterbalances your own tendencies; so if you are very results oriented, search for someone who is more people oriented, always with the proviso that it must be someone whose general competence you respect.

Having found this paragon of virtues, test your compatibility by describing the basic elements of your plan to him. As a coach he'll need the background anyway, and will be better equipped to observe you and provide valuable feedback. More important, by describing in detail what you're trying to accomplish you can get a better sense of your own willingness to be candid with this particular person and to utilize his help as you venture into the new territory outlined in your plan.

Having completed your plan and acquired an ally or two, you are now ready to get into action. Chapter 4 provides some suggestions for doing that safely and effectively.

4

Getting into Action

"There I was," Sally said to Frank, her husband and coach, "working hard at being my new reasonable self, when I completely lost it. I was patiently sitting in my office, listening to Terry blather on about how the new software wasn't as easy to use as the old and thinking to myself, 'For God sakes, stop whining and just learn to use it.' Then," Sally said with a sigh, "when Terry started in with, 'I told you it was a mistake to get a new statistical package,' I lost it. I blasted off with lecture number eighty-seven—I was leaning forward, probably glaring, the whole pontificating, self-righteous bit."

"So, what did you do to stop?" asked Frank.

"Thank you for the vote of confidence, Coach, but it was pretty clumsy. When I finally woke up to what I was doing, I just shut up and sat there and looked at my hands, my mind an absolute blank. Terry must have thought I was having a fit and finally got up and started out the door. So, I blurted out something like, 'Terry, what I meant is, I know it's hard, but keep working with it.' He didn't even stop. He just kept on going."

"Well, you may not have been very smooth about it," said Frank, "but at least you stopped yourself."

"You're probably right," she sighed. "I just wish I hadn't ended up looking like a fool. Maybe what I needed was a few dress rehearsals before I tried this behavior-change thing in real life."

Changing behavior patterns you've spent a lifetime perfecting is usually not as arduous a task as it may seem in anticipation, but it is hardly ever easy. First of all, you are trying to manage behavior that's been overlearned and heavily reinforced. Second, the old behavior made sense to you because it matched your feelings. After all, what is more sensible than losing your temper with someone who insists on whining about a decision that's already been made? Third, your recognition that you're doing just what you've chosen not to do is usually what cues you to switch to your more productive substitute behavior. So you are not only faced with carrying off a new response, but forced to do it, so to speak, in midconversation.

Thankfully, all of this improves with practice and the help of six valuable aids to modifying unwanted behavior: mental rehearsal, a stepwise approach to behavior control, co-opting others for support, handling the ups and downs of change, making repairs when you've slipped, and keeping an eye on how well you're doing.

USE MENTAL REHEARSAL

Mental rehearsal is a well-tested method for alleviating both the anticipatory nervousness and the clumsiness that accompany the learning of any new skill. The process by itself has a mixed parentage. On one side, it shares techniques with methods that are used to rid people of the rather common fears of snakes, spiders, and high places through the successive repetition in a safe atmosphere of mental images of what is feared. The methods work because mental images can often evoke the same kinds of physiological responses one would have in the actual situation.

Mental rehearsal's other parents are the well-supported findings that one can improve the performance of newly learned skills by imagining oneself practicing them over and over again. Not that mental rehearsal is a substitute for actual practice, but as Charles Garfield, who has studied peak performers in sports, business, and science, points out, visualizing demanding encounters significantly helps to improve performance and reduce inhibiting anxiety.

The nice thing about this process is that it helps whether you do it well or haphazardly. You'll gain some benefits by simply recalling a past interaction that didn't turn out well and, from your present perspective, by rewriting the script. For example, instead of having silently assented when your teammate said, "My plan is okay, right? Let's call it a day," you imagine yourself saying, "No! I'm uncomfortable with that," implementing your substitute behavioral response to surrendering when you feel overwhelmed.

However, you'll get extra benefits if you go about it more systematically. To do that, you'll start at the beginning by visualizing the physical setting in which your interaction is likely to occur. Now take yourself through each step of the event, starting with just the sort of situation that has led you into trouble in the past. As feelings arise, let them wash over you, then dissipate. Notice changes in your heart rate, breathing, and muscle tension, especially in those muscles to which you ordinarily displace fear or anger.

As you experience the feelings, use whatever aids to relaxation you've learned, or try deep breathing from the diaphragm with a slow exhalation. Then mentally proceed onto the next step until you've imagined yourself safely through the encounter.

Your sequence might start with an image of your staff stuck in an overly long silence, then a flaring of your temper. Perhaps someone teases you about your "playacting," and you see yourself losing control, becoming confused, but then falling back on one of your trusty substitute behaviors. If you lose your focus somewhere along the way, stop, relax a bit, then start again. Force yourself to go back over that dismal sequence several times until the happy ending begins to be boring. After all, isn't that what desensitization is all about?

STEPWISE BEHAVIOR CONTROL

Most difficult undertakings are best tackled one step at a time. For one thing, completing each step successfully gives you confidence to go on to the next. More important, you are less likely to feel overwhelmed if you have to keep your mind only on "What do I do next?" Stepwise behavior control is a technique that breaks the task of managing your unwanted behavior into eight discrete but related steps: recognize that you've slipped, put on the brakes, physically cue something new, shift to substitute behavior, identify precipitating factors, and carry out your change plan.

Realize You've Slipped

Unfortunately, just as Sally caught herself blasting out "lecture number eighty-seven," much of the time you will recognize that you've already slipped back into your old problem behavior. You might notice the superior tone to your voice or suddenly see your finger punching the air for emphasis right in someone's face. Perhaps you will be jarred by the realization of the defeated sound in your voice as you mumble, "Yes, I'll do it," when you know you should be saying, "No, it's just not possible."

At times, your transition into your difficult mode may be so subtle that the recognition will be cued more by the reactions of others than by your own awareness of your feelings or behavior. Here is an example:

> James Tillson was a generally successful professor of English who had been startled to find that student evaluators had described him in this way: "sometimes interesting, sometimes boring, occasionally pontificates." After eliciting feedback from his spouse and a rather brave teaching assistant, he was able to pin down what in his teaching style led to those comments. He not only answered questions posed by a student, but also proceeded to lecture that student, and therefore the rest of the class, about the background and general ideology of the topic raised by the question. Professor Tillson found it most difficult to detect

the point at which he moved from well-rounded answer to surfeit of knowledge, interesting to him but irrelevant to the class. But by keeping an eye on several particularly responsive students whom he had learned to identify earlier in the semester, he could see signs that "sometimes interesting" was turning into "sometimes boring." He was then able to move on to step number two, putting on the brakes.

Putting On the Brakes

At the instant you realize that your difficult behavior has come into play, bring yourself to a sudden halt. Break off the behavior—in midsentence, if necessary. Even at the risk of creating that awful, unexplainable pause in the interaction that so puzzled Sally's employee, simply stop what you're doing. Remember that you are attempting to gain control over habitual, well-entrenched behavior, prodded by a variety of strong emotions and often rationalized as being appropriate to the situation—for example, "He deserves to be yelled at."

Fancy footwork at this stage can easily get out of hand and leave you even more emotionally overloaded—a recipe for impulsive, inappropriate behavior. In that circumstance, the simplest way to gain control is to stop doing and saying anything. In practice, you'll try to find some socially acceptable way to interrupt your behavior. One saving grace is the fact that most people are made uncomfortable by silence, and they will leap into the breach and fill it with their own jabber, giving you a few seconds to move to the next helpful step, physically cuing your substitute behavior.

Physically Cuing Your Substitute Behavior

You may find it of considerable help to reinforce your control with some kind of simple physical behavior. Examples that I've seen work are touching the crystal of a wristwatch, touching a favorite pen, touching or surreptitiously knocking on wood (that centuries-old warder-off of misfortune), yogic (from the diaphragm) breathing, touching an earlobe, or pushing eyeglasses farther up the bridge of the nose (yes, in pre-tobacco-prohibition days, the act of lighting pipes and cigarettes served the physical-cuing function rather well).

Such actions serve a number of purposes. They provide a relief from the tension of the moment. They mark an important event—namely, you've gained control over unwanted behavior, you *do something* that adds to your sense of being in control. These actions also remind you to move on to the next step, tossing out whatever substitute behaviors you've thought up as part of your plan.

More important, planned physical mannerisms help prevent a strange phenomenon that bedevils people who have decided *not* to do something. An embarrassingly frequent experience ("I won't, I won't, I won't spill wine on the rug,—oops!") highlights a frustrating irony in attempts at mental control: an intense concentration on *not* behaving in a certain way can set you up for the exact behavior that you are trying to squelch. This effect is more likely to occur when you're trying hard not to do something while under a mental or emotional load—exactly the circumstance you're likely to be in when your difficult behavior emerges. By refocusing your mind on some simple physical action that momentarily relieves your cognitive load, you lessen the chance that, while deploring the fact that you just one-upped your teammate, you'll find yourself one-upping him again.

Shift to Substitute Behavior

Having shut up and stabilized yourself by touching your watch, you're once again in charge and ready to rejoin the flow of events with the substitute behaviors you've devised in your plan. At least that's the theory. However, in the firefight, things may not go quite as planned. A furious Sally had completely lost track of her planned substitute behavior ("How can I help you?") and, for doubtlessly too long, found herself unable to say anything at all.

Lesson#1: If you lose your way in this one-step-at-a-time process, stick with silence. Sure, her obnoxious employee Terry, not knowing what else to do, started to leave and may not have heard Sally's last-minute attempt at sounding sensible, but she had achieved a first victory, learning to regain control and cut her losses.

Which leads us to *Lesson #2:* Any substitute response will help to move your change effort along, even if it isn't as smooth as you'd like it to be. Sally's "What I meant, Terry . . ." wasn't superb, but it gave her confidence that she could respond to a confrontational situation with something other than word bashing. Suppose Sally's silence had lasted until Terry had completely left the room; would that have been a significant setback? Absolutely not! As we'll see in more detail later in the chapter, all substantial change efforts, including the most successful, undergo ups and downs.

Identify Precipitating Factors

As soon as possible after your unwanted behavior has surfaced, try to find some quiet moments in which you can review what just happened, to pinpoint as specifically as possible the events and feelings that preceded your difficult behavior. Do you recognize one of the personal-threat situations that you identified in developing your plan? How did you feel just before the impulse to behave in the old way hit you? The clearer you are about how the connection between your feelings and your behavior works, the better able you will be to head that behavior off before it becomes full blown. Mere insight into your emotionally vulnerable points does not immediately insulate you from their effects. But awareness of them can alert you that your favorite defensive behavior may be following close behind.

Sally had identified an unreasonably strong antipathy toward anyone who "whined instead of working." Although she saw the connection between her know-it-all dismissal of her staff's objections and their complaining, her insight about the degree to which she had brought on just the behavior that provoked her the most did not immediately stop the complaining. Nonetheless, Sally was certain that she would no longer be subject to those sudden fits of righteous anger.

Unfortunately, she was wrong. Certainly, she had underestimated Terry's skill at sounding just the right whining note with impeccable timing, and "lecture number eighty-seven" rumbled into action once again. Discouraging as it was, Sally benefited from her first, somewhat shaky attempt to manage her tendency toward verbal overkill. She realized that the task would require more serious attention than she'd previously thought. This time, when I suggested that she try a little mental rehearsal before she next went into action, she listened.

Carry Out Your Change Plan

Up until now, your effort has been to rein in an old troublesome behavior and replace it with words and actions that, while consistent with your style and purpose, are better tuned to your developmental goals. Having gained confidence in your ability to use your substitute behaviors when you need to, you must now review the other elements in your plan and bring to bear those that seem appropriate. Perhaps your plan calls for you to change your staff meeting format, participate in training in active listening, or change your apparel to match your new behavior.

The one certainty about human learning is that its course will always be uneven. Even in the simplest kinds of rote learning—memorizing sequences of numbers, say—initially rapid progress will dip when subjects are pushed to learn lengthier number sequences, then rise to new peaks until they reach a point where they seemingly can't stretch their memories any further. Even then, after a rest followed by much (boring) practice, some subjects' learning curves may yet creep a bit upward. With the kind of far more complex learning events—actually unlearning events—we're addressing here, the learning ups and downs are even more dramatic. Not only will your initial trials be plagued by the clumsiness of any self-conscious effort, you will very likely be in for occasional setbacks and relapses, as the old, overlearned and well-reinforced behaviors persist in intruding, often just when you believe that you've finally eradicated them forever.

HANDLING THE UPS AND DOWNS OF CHANGE

Here are some key diary entries from Sally's first few weeks at her self-management task:

September 6: Blew up at Terry, then salvaged it, sort of.

September 9: Staff meeting, Mort's report on the Ridewell Customer Survey. His analysis incomplete. Bit my tongue. Made appointment with him for tomorrow.

September 13: Started to "inform" Jack (national sales manager) of basics of focus groups. Saw his impatience. Ended with, "Well, you know focus groups as well as I do." Got a smile.

September 21: Threw pencil across table when Terry brought up new software. Said, "Sorry—thought we'd finished all that. How can I help?" He looked cowed anyway. I probably looked grim. Tough!!

September 23: Lectured at staff meeting for twenty minutes. Damn!! Sheri asked, "Are you sore at us, Sally?" I mumbled and we ended the meeting.

October 1: Terry bitched about new program again. I felt the old hackles rise but just said, "How can I help you, Terry?" He stated a specific—I referred him to Mary (in the MIS Division). Victory!!

October 9 (Saturday): Call at home from my boss—where is monthly report? Told him to ask his stupid secretary. Silence. Finally said, "I mean, I put it on her desk Friday about four thirty." Silence. I said, "Have a nice weekend," and hung up.

October 11: Checked with boss that he'd gotten my report. He had. He said (door was closed), "She may be stupid, but she's all I've got." I apologized. He said, "I know you've been trying, Sally; mostly it's working. Keep it up."

Here are some suggestions for handling these ubiquitous ups and downs of change.

Like Sally, at times you'll find your new substitute behaviors ready on your tongue, easing you through the same situations in which you were formerly aroused, confused, or oblivious. However, it's also likely that you'll have your Terrys, whose simple existence will pull from you the very behaviors you're trying so hard to manage. Since your reaction to those victories and especially to the inevitable setbacks can affect your commitment to your program, it is critical to understand why progress is usually uneven and how to keep from being sidetracked by both the ups and downs.

You might think of them as pitfalls to which you'll stay alert, to be avoided when possible, and to be clambered out of when they're not, never distracting you from the path that in time will make the new behavior as much a part of you as was the old. The most common hazards are derisive banter from others, overly optimistic assessment of how you're doing, impatience with the slow pace of change, a perfectionist reaction to routine slips and setbacks, hidden fears that you might actually improve, stress overload, and lack of appreciation.

Derisive Banter

One of the fascinating aspects of any sort of personal change program is the way friends, family members, and colleagues— often those who complained the most about the old behavior— will mobilize to attack the changes that have been made. About two months into Sally's behavior-management program, this conversation ensued between her and, as you might expect, Terry, her complaining subordinate:

> TERRY: What's with this "how can I help" bit, anyway? I'm trying to have a conversation. Is that what they taught you at that charm school last year?
> SALLY: Damn it, Terry . . . What I mean is just what I said— what do you need from me right now?
> TERRY: Well, it's nice to see there's still life in you, Sally.
> SALLY: I just decided that snapping at a lot of people all the time wasn't getting me anywhere.
> TERRY: You know, it didn't take a genius to see that you weren't really being yourself. Forget all this psychologizing stuff and just go back to being the Sally we loved to get pissed at.

One should admire competence whenever it's displayed. With the sure hand of an expert, Terry had exposed Sally as a blundering charlatan who had been conned into trying a charm school technique on her loyal and hardworking staff. (The "charm school" Terry referred to was a management-training course Sally had attended in the previous year, in which she had learned much about managing resources and little about managing people.) Sally later reported that she had suffered through a night of alternating shame and anger directed equally at Terry, her boss, and me for getting her into this snake pit. When we met, a week after her "counseling" from Terry, she was still confused.

"Perhaps he was right," she wondered. "What I'm trying to do sure is artificial."

"Was doing what came naturally better?" I queried.

"I hate it when you do that—you're so smug—but, no it wasn't better, and saying, 'How can I help,' did stop that little bastard's complaining, artificial or not."

"Of course," I said, probably sounding smug again, "why do you think he gave you the treatment? It sounds like it almost worked."

Why did Terry try to trash what he should have welcomed? Such reactions to positive change in others have been repeatedly observed in the families of those recovering from mental illness ("We just wanted her to stop seeing things, but now that pushy psychiatrist has her insisting she wants to run her own life."). It's also a common reaction to those who try for significant change in their personal-care habits ("Losing weight is fine, George, but that's no reason to become compulsive about dieting. Live a little.").

The most obvious reason for these "friendly" shoves back into quicksand comes from the interactional and systemic nature of human relationships. If you change in some significant way, your altered behavior will inevitably exert pressure on me to change in some way. My options will be to complement your change with one of my own, to resist, or—clearly the most efficient route—to push you back to being your good old annoying self. One does not have to be too astute to see that as Sally became less of an explosive know-it-all, her subordinates would need much more creative ways to excuse their own failings.

Overly Optimistic Assessment of How You're Doing

Rex was district manager for a household-products corporation that had committed itself to employee empowerment and teamwork. After months of whispered complaints about Rex's poor management, the regional manager to whom he reported sat him down with the seven members of his sales team for an open feedback session. Rex was genuinely surprised to find that he was seen as distant and un-supportive, that he played favorites with the two salespeo-ple that he had known the longest, that he never solicited ideas on how to resolve difficult district problems, and that he himself was so personally disorganized that notes and memos sent to him were often never acknowledged.

In his favor, all of the staff members saw him as excep-tionally capable in handling difficult customer problems, a buffer between themselves and upper management who leaned over backwards to overlook or minimize mistakes made by any member of the sales staff (his boss was not quite so sure this was a positive).

Having gotten the word, Rex set out to change his be-havior, and, having done so, he assumed that his failings had been adequately addressed. However, six months later, confidential interviews ordered by senior management in-formed his boss that although Rex was seen to have initially tried to communicate better, he had soon reverted to his old ways. He was shocked and puzzled. "Not one person on my staff complained to me about any of this stuff, even though I asked them at every sales meeting how things were going," he told me later. "I really made an effort. What went wrong?"

Rex was not an obtuse man; few salespeople are. But like most successful people in that line of work, he viewed the world with a bias toward happy endings. While this is generally a most satis-factory way to maintain a sunny emotional tone, at times it leads to overconfident interpretations and a tendency to induce con-firming responses to support that rosy view ("I'm listening more now, aren't I?").

From my own interviews with the sales staff, conducted dur-ing the "one last chance," six-month probation period Rex ne-gotiated, it seemed clear that initially he had made some significant changes in his behavior and that these had been no-ticed and appreciated by his staff. However, after a month or so, confident that he had things under control, Rex's attention had drifted to other matters, and he became oblivious to the signs that he had slipped back into his old behavior patterns.

His lack of awareness was not the product solely of ordinary forgetfulness or the refocus of attention to job demands. Through the luck of the genetic draw, he happened to be what environmental psychologist Albert Mehrabian calls a "high screener," one whose perceptual apparatus tends to screen out the subtle early-warning signs that a crisis is about to hit. As Mehrabian has shown, people vary considerably in their sensitivity to what's going on around and inside them. For example, if you are a manager or if in your work you deal more with things than people, the odds are good that you are a higher screener than those around you. If so, you'll need to stay particularly alert to taking too optimistic a view of how well you're doing, especially four to six weeks after you've begun your change program, when you feel confident that you've rather quickly done all that anyone could expect of you. Otherwise, like Rex, you may abruptly discover that altering old patterns is not quite the simple task you thought it would be.

Impatience with the Slow Pace of Change

Because it involves unlearning the old as well as gaining skill with the new, your program is likely to take too much time, or it will certainly seem so—especially if you are one of those energetic, task-oriented individuals who likes everything done expeditiously and on schedule. While impatience may get you started without the hesitation that plagues some would-be behavior remodelers, it can also push you to expect results too quickly, and you can find yourself too quickly disappointed and ready to chuck the whole program. Don't. Remind yourself that real change takes time. If it is too rapid it usually turns out to be superficial and short lived.

Perfectionist Reactions to Slips and Setbacks

Most people accept missteps and setbacks as a natural consequence of learning, and if they're wise, they find in these mishaps exactly the information that can help them move toward their goals. However, for some people, often those of high ability, the only truly acceptable goal is perfection, and anything short of that signifies failure. A rather charming, if ironic, tribute to the persistence of a perfectionist view is unintentionally rendered by those clients who, finally convinced that making and learning from mistakes is indeed a mark of champions, set out to attain a perfect absence of perfectionism. It is testimony to the complexity of the human mind that they often ruefully see the predicament in which their perfectionism had placed them, even while pursuing it.

A usually effective remedy for perfectionist tendencies has been best articulated by Albert Ellis and other rational-emotive therapists. It has the following steps:

Step 1. Spend some introspective time identifying the beliefs that drive your perfectionism. Then divide a piece of paper (or your computer screen) into three equal columns and write the beliefs in the lefthand column. They will look something like this:

> I must perform this and all other important tasks without mistakes or errors or I'm a failure (inferior, a no-goodnick, "just like your father, or mother, or uncle Harry"), and I can't stand thinking I might be that way.

Step 2. In the center column, alongside that somewhat nonsensical belief, write a disputation of it. It might look like this:

> Where is the evidence that mistakes are sinful rather than just events to be corrected and learned from, that I *must* be perfect in everything, and that if I'm not always perfect, I'm a failure?

Step 3. In the righthand column rewrite your original belief, leaving out the nonsense:

> I would prefer not to make mistakes, because they cause extra effort and can sometimes be costly, but I now realize that the only way to never make a mistake is to never try anything new, a price I am unwilling to pay. It's also clear to me that the people I most admire often make mistakes and are therefore imperfect, yet they are neither failures nor inferior.

Even if you suffer from only the mildest form of perfectionism, keep alert to fleeting thoughts that there's no hope since you've slipped once or twice, so you might as well stop trying. If you catch one of these sabotaging doubts darting through your mind, jot it down, smile a little, and then reprise the preceding exercise.

Hidden Fears That You Might Actually Improve

Have you repeatedly postponed getting started on your program or, having taken the first few steps, do you wonder why you embarked on this silly self-improvement project at all? If so, resist for a moment the impulse to mumble, "They'll just have to take me as I am," jettison your notes, and consign this book to your next garage sale. Instead, commit yourself to one last spasm of note taking. Imagine and then write down all of the harms that could come your way if your difficult behavior should actually disappear. Be as creative as you can.

Here are some of the more interesting statements that clients have come up with in answer to the question "What are the dangers if you improve?"

- "If I'm no longer seen as brilliant but unstable, I'll finally be made a section head and have to deal with people, something I've always hated."

- "If I become more decisive, I'll have to live with my decisions, which is scary because I'm sometimes wrong."

- "If I stop cracking jokes all the time, I'll be boring."

- "If I don't tell them everything I know about the subject, they won't know how smart I am."

Were these hidden fears the real reasons for their authors' procrastination, irritation, or boredom? It's certainly likely that they played some part, but it's also equally likely that they were buttressed by and intertwined with other, perhaps deeper, motivational threads that would take more than ten minutes of solitary thinking to uncover. But it doesn't matter. The simple act of looking for inner resistances often enables many people to continue to pursue the goals they've set for themselves.

Stress Overload

Unfortunately, your decision to manage some aspect of your difficult behavior does not guarantee that the fates will keep their grubby hands off you while you pursue that worthwhile goal. An incendiary customer crisis, rumors of an impending merger, a wildcat strike that cuts off income, or an ill child or rebellious teenager are just a few of the life events that can overload your capacity for cool, effective action. Many of these events will *not* overwhelm you emotionally, and you will be able to remain calm, thoughtful, and in charge of your behavior. But when crises like these also tap your inner insecurities, it is likely that your control will become a little ragged, unleashing those old troublesome patterns. Don't wait for that to happen. When you become aware that your ability to cope has been stretched too thin, try one of these short-term courses of action. First try refocusing your behavior control on a very basic level: at the first signs that you may be slipping (shrill voice, jabbing finger), close your mouth, sit back, and wait for calm. If that control measure isn't working well enough, a second line of defense is to inform those most affected that you are on edge or feeling a little moody, so that they will understand that your temper is your problem (and you know it), not simply the result of their misdeeds.

Lack of Appreciation

Like Sally, you have worked your change well for six weeks, feel the satisfying pride of accomplishment, and now wait expectantly for at least a few claps on the back. Nice thought, but don't count on it. Your wish for a few "well done's" is certainly understandable—true achievement hungers for recognition. Unhappily, it may be a while before improvements you're aware of are noticed by others. For one thing, others are too full of their own lives to notice much about yours, unless you are causing them real discomfort. *Lack* of discomfort, the result of your successful efforts, often goes unnoticed until attention is dramatically called to it.

Then, too, those who feel they have been in some way hurt by your past behavior may see the changes not as an improvement so much as a return to normalcy ("I should compliment him that he's no longer beating up on me?").

Finally, there's the problem that you're a human being and therefore imperfect. As a self-rehabilitated indecisive, for example, you may take strong positions on eight of the next ten issues that come to your attention, but when you equivocate on the last two—after all, only compulsive control freaks are decisive all the time—it may be taken as evidence that you haven't really changed much at all or that the change was only temporary and cosmetic.

We will revisit these issues in Chapter 5, when we consider the best methods for changing your image. The main point here is that you may have to provide your own "well done's", perhaps with the help of your coach.

Paradoxically, the greatest help to remaining on course is expecting to be occasionally thrown off. Anticipating trouble can help in several ways.

Expect the Inevitable

If you have accepted the fact that occasional regressions are a usual part of a change program, especially when the targets of change are difficult to hit, you'll be less surprised when they do occur, which is a real benefit because unexpected stumbles are always more stressful than those you have anticipated. To that end, remind yourself of potential pitfalls by a quick review of this section about a month after the start of your program.

The main thing to remember is to view occasional lapses as normal, particularly if you have perfectionist tendencies. The alternative, a discouraged feeling that you have failed forever— rather than faltered briefly and inconsequentially—can seriously disrupt your progress.

Work Your Plan

Much of the power of twelve-step programs comes from their emphasis on maintaining the same consistent program, regardless of whether one is moving forward or sliding back. Their basic premise, "Whether things are going well or not, work your program," is sound advice for anyone embarked on any sort of behavior change, if only because it keeps you active even during moments of discouragement. One simple way to do that is to periodically review the basic elements of your plan to remind yourself why you embarked on this painful journey in the first place.

CO-OPT OTHERS FOR SUPPORT

In Chapter 3, I suggested identifying a coach to help you reconcile the varying perspectives of your informants and think through your change plan. That same person might also be your best source of perspective and comfort when you must weather occasional lapses. Your mutual goals should be both propping up your sense of your own efficacy and renewing your commitment if your enthusiasm or energy are flagging a bit.

Carefully consider the possibility, when it is feasible, of enlisting your boss, subordinates, teammates, spouse, or close friends as allies in your effort to become a more well-rounded or skillful person. Share with them your commitment, mention target behaviors that you've initially decided to give priority to, and ask for feedback on how well you're doing. Suggest to them how and when you'd prefer to receive the feedback. Even if their intention is to be helpful, keep in mind that you'll probably not want seven people letting you know just how well or poorly you've done every time you open your mouth. Check with them from time to time on how effective your substitute behaviors are, and whether your nonverbal behavior is consistent with your new skills. Ease their discomfort about commenting on your personal appearance, facial expressions, and gestures by reminding them that you are the only one who can't see your face in action.

Several important advantages accrue from enlisting others as allies. When you slip, it will be seen as such, an unintended loss of control for which you can be forgiven. Recall that it is the imputed intention behind an act, not the act itself, that determines whether or not it arouses blame or sympathetic understanding.

A less obvious benefit to acknowledging your awareness of personal liabilities, along with a positive plan for ameliorating them, is an almost invariable rise in the esteem with which you will be held. Psychologists call it taking a one-down position—openly admitting to your human imperfections—and point out that doing so is seen by others as a sign of strength. It is a tactic often put to good use by successful negotiators.

One of the most formidable chief financial officers that I have known made his entry into important contract negotiations with, "It's probably just that this kind of technical issue is too much for me, but would somebody please explain why . . . ?" After the issue had been patiently explained, he would proceed to point out what his company had to have if agreement were to be reached. When I later chided him about the frequent use of this tactic and other self-deprecating terms (his other favorite was "I may be nothing but an overeducated farm boy, but . . ."), he admitted to his manipulative intent but insisted it was not "to put something over on anybody." He had discovered, he said, that given his position in a Fortune 100 company, no one ever really believed that he was incompetent, but "putting myself down seems to relax everybody, so that when it's time to settle things, they don't try to squeeze more out of me than they should."

Through the years, my observation has certainly been that when you tell coworkers that you recognize a need for development and that you intend to pursue it, they often wish that they could be equally courageous, calm, and confident.

Whether to enlist your boss as a coach deserves careful thought. Bosses often lack the opportunity to directly observe those they supervise in action, so they rely on a mix of personal impressions developed in face-to-face conversations or staff meetings, objective data, and customer and employee complaints or compliments to make judgments about performance quality and promotional potential. To the extent that your boss fits that description, you might be better off keeping her as an interested observer, rather than suggesting a coaching role. Coaches are most valuable when they can directly observe you during those times when your difficult behavior is most likely to surface. Those who coach at a distance are likely to provide general advice—usually of little benefit—rather than the specific feedback and ideas for modifying your substitute behaviors that can be so useful.

If you feel a certain reluctance when you contemplate involving your boss, subordinates, and (especially) peers as active participants in your change program, you'll have much company. "They'll see my imperfections," "They'll laugh at me," "I'll just provide ammunition to those who are out to get me," and "It'll be blabbed all over the whole company" are all doubts that have been voiced to me by clients who were committed to handling their troublesome behavior but thought it should be a private affair. For most, taking the first small step of discussing their plans with one particularly trusted individual made further sharing a somewhat less jarring prospect.

MAKING REPAIRS WHEN YOU'VE SLIPPED

About two months after she had started her program, Sally's unit was hit by a product-modification crisis, necessitating more than two weeks of fourteen-hour workdays. By the twelfth day, the need for broad-gauged thinking and offbeat ideas that had initially energized the team had given way to the exactingly tedious individual work of double-checking data entries and careful documentation. Given her own anxiety about whether the new product would meet an important customer's needs, it was, perhaps, understandable that Sally lost sight of two important facts: that stress might lessen her control over her bulldozing impulses if she were crossed and that general fatigue and twelve days of bad coffee had correspondingly eroded her staff's ability to cope with her.

The excitement began when Sally asked Sheri, her brightest product designer, to recheck her final computer run for the third time. Sheri, who had a temper of her own, shot back, "If you had paid more attention to our questions when we first started on this stupid product, we wouldn't have had to spend all this time keeping your ass out of the wringer." The escalating dialogue ended with Sally resoundingly lecturing all those present—and several passersby—that they had to learn to speak up if they had doubts, and if they didn't, they deserved whatever they got.

"I really screwed up," Sally told Frank later that night. "First of all, I knew I was losing it even before it happened. I was sitting in a corner brooding over a cup of coffee, and I had a vision of trying to explain to an already pissed-off customer why the software we'd spent all this time and money on wasn't working. And the next thing I knew, I was nudging Sheri to recheck it. Then when she turned on me, I never even thought of my crutch phrase, 'That's an interesting view; let's discuss it later.'"

"Well," said Frank. "Now you can practice your damage control techniques. When and where can you get back with Sheri?"

Not all relapses are equally important. Like the concert musician whose appreciation of what the audience took to be a first-rate performance is marred by his awareness of minor mistakes, you'll be aware of many slips unrecognized by those with whom you're working. Some episodes of difficult behavior, however, are worth at least a modicum of damage control, both to keep the interactional fires from spreading and because follow-up on your part will increase the probability that next time you'll stop yourself before your control point has been breached.

Although repairing a rift in a relationship is hardly ever pleasant—that's the negative reinforcement that acts as a future preventive—it needn't be impossibly burdensome. Repair has three essential steps: acknowledging that regardless of the situation, your behavior was not constructive; stating your regret that the other person was discomfited by that behavior; and suggesting steps that should preclude a repetition of the untoward event. Here is Sally's version of how she handled the repair with her subordinate Sheri:

SALLY (poking her head into Sheri's office): Can I have five minutes, Sheri?

SHERI (not looking up): I guess.

SALLY (sitting down): What I did at the meeting yesterday was way out of bounds. That stupid lecture that I dumped on everyone was bad enough, but insisting that you, of all people, recheck all your work when I knew that you'd already rechecked it twice was plain dumb. I know that being stubborn about things like that has been getting in my way, and

I'm trying to stop it, but I sure didn't do it last night.

SHERI: You sure didn't!

SALLY: Sounds like it's given you some bad moments. I'm really sorry about that.

SHERI (turning slowly to look directly at Sally): To tell you the truth, Sally, I've been sitting here thinking about taking that Burrow's Company job offer. After you left last night, everybody else just came down on me for pushing your buttons. What really bothered me was your lecturing them when you were really mad at me. And maybe I am to blame for not trying harder to stop you. If that's the case, I'm not sure that I want to go to the trouble.

SALLY: You know, Sheri, what's so awful about this is that I've finally realized that I've been getting in my own way by not paying attention to what smart people like you have to say, and that my lecturing, which I always thought was simply me being logical, is a real turnoff. Anyway, what I would like to ask you to do—if you're willing—when you think I'm not paying attention to what's being said to me, interrupt me and say, "Sally, just listen." I'm not trying to put the responsibility on you, you understand; it's up to me to pay attention, and mostly, I think, I've been getting better at it. But I just don't want to slide back into my old ways.

SHERI: Do you really mean that? I mean about my saying, "Just listen"? You always sound so positive, and you're so full of reasons why you're right. I know you told everyone last night, meaning me especially, that we should speak up more, but you just don't know how much of a bulldozer you can be.

SALLY (ruefully): Well, I'm finding out pretty fast, and as I said, I don't like it. Yes, I absolutely mean what I said about interrupting, and if it doesn't work the first time, say it again.

SHERI: You know, that might be fun. Can I tell the others about it?

SALLY: Well, I'm thinking about talking about my new development plan at the next staff meeting, so I'd rather you didn't say anything. After all, I don't want to sound like a wimp.

SHERI: Sally, you will never, ever sound like a wimp.

Some repair jobs need not be quite this elaborate. If her outburst had not been quite so loud, subtly insulting, or public, Sally might only have needed to acknowledge her lapsed behavior and chat with Sheri about a more thorough interactive discussion at their next planning meeting.

A caution about apologies: While they are useful social devices for showing lack of intent to do harm, when they take the form "I'm sorry I made you feel bad," apologies can have some confusing effects. You are not only taking responsibility for the other person's feelings but may induce the person who was the target of your behavioral lapse into saying, "Oh, that's all right," when it isn't all right at all, thereby increasing hidden resentment, just what you're trying to prevent. In contrast, a simple statement of regret that the other person has had a bad time of it doesn't require that the injured party lie to make you feel better. In fact, one purpose for your acknowledgment, in addition to showing that you recognize that you did something that you, yourself, deemed inappropriate, is to provoke more information about the impact your behavior had, rather than shutting it off.

Keep an Eye On How Well You're Doing

A common characteristic of well-laid plans, especially those that involve people, is that they always need adjustment. So occasionally checking on how well your plan is working is a wise move.

To monitor how faithfully you are implementing your plan and determine how well it is serving your needs, ask yourself these questions:

- What seems to be working well? What is not? How am I feeling?

- Am I actually doing what my plan called for? For example, did I stop what I was saying when I noticed my impatience, or was I too embarrassed about acting strangely?

- Do my substitute behaviors need modification or more practice? Are the phrases so complicated and hard to say that I get tongue tied? Perhaps they are out of sync with the situation in which I'm trying to use them. For example, one client told this story: "'I'll check it out with my financial people and get back to you' seemed like an ideal substitute to counter my tendency to make thoughtless promises to customers ('Sure, we can do it for three thousand dollars'). But now I find that while my substitute behavior keeps me from giving away the store, it turns some potential customers off."

- Have I stumbled into the common pitfalls that are outlined in this chapter?

- Would more mental rehearsal or skill practice with a coach or mentor be helpful? How can I arrange for that?

- Would a training course be helpful? One, for example, on how to communicate assertively rather than hostilely or indirectly?

In addition to informing whatever plan reshaping you'll need to do, your answers to questions like these will provide useful material for discussions with your coach or mentor. Even more important, they can serve as a valuable antidote for the querulous doubts that are likely to plague even the hardiest of self-developers, such as "Why do I have to do all this stuff?" "Haven't I done enough already?" "Why can't I postpone this exercise until I'm not so busy?"

Maintenance over the Long Haul

After a time—perhaps as soon as two months, usually by six months, occasionally by two years—your courage, your dogged persistence, and your saving sense of humor will pay off: comments may come from those you care about that you've changed; employees who previously stayed out of your way until necessity required their presence will begin to seek you out; you hear yourself give direct and unvarnished feedback to a problem employee; or you stand up to your problem boss. Enjoy your glow of quiet pride, give a relieved sigh that the travail is behind you, and begin to consider where else to turn your attentions.

Remind yourself, however, to check out your behavioral health periodically. While there is good evidence that over time a change in behavior produces changes in attitude and outlook, it does take time.

True, some behavioral improvements tend to be self-maintaining. For example, an increase in friendly overtures because you are less self-aggrandizing boosts your ego, so you have less need to boast, which makes you more likeable, which . . . But others can resurface, especially during stressful times. Be particularly watchful that you do not once more begin to overuse your best attributes—again avoiding necessary confrontations when you're feeling resentful that your sacrifice has gone unappreciated. The uncomfortable truth is that without occasional propping up, your old troublesome behavior may once again get in your way.

To be sure, it will not be easy to keep your eye on past failings. You've plenty of other more enjoyable things to do, and the normal tendency to forget the bad and remember the good will conspire to keep your attention elsewhere. However, one way to trick yourself into occasionally remembering to check up on yourself is to leave a copy of your development plan in a place where you can't avoid seeing it from time to time. The middle desk drawer may be a possibility. The front of your calendar is another. Sure, in time it too will likely fade into the background. Still, there is also a chance—my experience deems it a good chance—that at least once a year, you'll flip through it and remind yourself to once again notice the effects of your behavior.

It is irksome, but unfortunately true, that once one's reputation has been blackened, it is sometimes difficult to rub off the tarnish, even when the causes have been removed. Having successfully modified your behavior, you can be enormously frustrated to find that you are still talked about as if you have not changed at all, not only by those who are not in a position to judge you day to day, but sometimes even by those who are. If that grossly unjust state of affairs should come to your attention, curse the fates loudly, but then accept the fact that you have an image problem. Like it or not, you'll need to deal with it as a separate issue. Thankfully, there is a rather well-tested method for doing just that. In the next chapter, we'll explore ways to change a negative image so that it will not interfere with promotions, interesting assignments, and the other benefits to which your hard work has now entitled you.

5

Repairing Your Image

Nicole Bonnet couldn't believe what her boss had just told her. "What do you mean I didn't get the supervising parole officer job? I'm sure as hell better qualified than Mel Franks, who got it. I was number one on the supes list. I've had three commendations as a grade-two parole officer. I've even been shot at."

"I know," said Sol, her boss, "and you *should* be pissed. The reason you weren't picked—to tell the truth—is about as stupid as it could get. You were blackballed by Danny Corbett, our esteemed deputy director for community services, who—"

"But, he hasn't even seen me for five years, since he was the regional parole chief and I was a rookie."

"Yeah, kid, but he still remembers that you were pretty disorganized then, and he especially remembers the time you violated that parolee who turned out to be—for once—innocent. You hadn't checked your facts, and you let your feelings run away with you. Danny was embarrassed before the parole board, and he hasn't forgotten."

"But didn't you tell him—"

"Sure, I told him and the other members of the promotion board. But you know Danny; he's smooth as silk. He
didn't say anything bad about you, he just said you were
'not quite ready.' And anyway, I'm only a supe grade two,
and he's a deputy director. What we have to do, Nicki, is
plan how we're going keep this from happening again."

It's unfair, but sometimes negative impressions remain in the
minds of others long after the flaws or foibles on which they
were based are well contained and of little consequence. In this
chapter, we'll look briefly at why jaundiced impressions hang on
so long, and then move on to the steps that work admirably well
to repair a damaged image.

WHY ISN'T CHANGING ENOUGH?

You've changed for the better. You no longer postpone conflict-
evoking decisions. No more do you deliver lectures when others
expect conversations. Or, like Nicole, you were once a disorganized hipshooter, but now, while still creative, you are a practical
enough planner to check facts. Surely those differences will be
plain to everyone.

Well, sometimes they are. Those who have paid close attention
to your developmental efforts, the people who work closely with
you, and supporters who are looking for improvements will notice first, especially if you tell them that you believe you've
changed. Often, however, in the minds of some important people,
you will exist only as an old stereotype, stuck in a box labeled "indecisive," "know-it-all," or "disorganized and immature." Worse,
you may find out about it only when, like Nicole, you are passed
over for promotion or your name appears on the short lay-off list.

While you may be infuriated and depressed to discover that
powerful executives, clients, or customers are prejudging you on
the basis of irrelevant criteria, you must move beyond those feelings to do what's necessary to break the stereotype. Understanding why such stereotypes persist may help you avoid becoming
immobilized by anger or hopeless resignation.

The basic problem is that we human beings perceive the world
by matching what we see against a vast number of stored holo-

graphic "photos"—psychologists call them *schemas*—and when one of these schemas fits the situation pretty well, the picture becomes our reality. It's easy to see why our nervous systems evolved this way, because this sort of automatic thinking is very efficient, and it works most of the time. When it doesn't—that is, when there's a poor fit between the stored picture and the specifics of the real situation—we're usually not aware of it unless the mismatch leads to serious consequences.

For example, if we label our neighbor's occasionally seen dog as friendly, we will very likely not notice that the animal is becoming grouchier with age until, when visiting, we are nipped. Even then we may explain the first few nips as "odd" and "not like him." If they continue, however, we will then marvel that the pup has turned vicious. Having newly relabeled the poor dog, we will fail to notice when the dog regains his original friendliness because the vet's arthritis treatments have kicked in.

Since those whose judgments you care about will be well equipped with this same "change reality to fit the stored mental image" perceptual software, it will be an image of the old you that crosses their minds when they think about you, until something happens to recast that image.

Unfortunately, image disconfirming is not always a simple affair. For one thing, the person whose image you'd like changed—a senior manager, say—will need to pay reasonably close attention to the details of your new behavioral style. However, high-status people tend to pay demonstrably less attention to the behavior of those lower in the social hierarchy, so that small discrepancies between the way you are now acting and the way those important others expect you to act are likely to be ignored. (The reverse is also true, which is why those you supervise will notice changes in your behavior before your boss does.)

A second complication is that even occasional and inconsequential lapses are often taken as proof that you haven't really changed. Deputy Director Corbett, Nicole's nemesis, had actually heard some good things about her recent work. In the five years since she had been jarred by Sol's comment "Shape up, kid, or they'll ship you back to the slammer"—where Nicole had been a preparole counselor—she had tempered her ability to relate to tough parolees with a constructive attention to fact finding and detailed documentation. She had been promoted to the highest working-parole-officer level, a move that did not require approval by the agency brass. Yet one minor incident, six months prior to the promotional competition, had confirmed Corbett's picture of her as irresponsible.

While attending a seminar at the agency headquarters, Nicole joined in with a group of fellow participants to plan a dinner party at a local restaurant. Corbett, who had been a workshop presenter, had also been invited. Whether Nicole was truly a victim of someone else's too-sketchy communication about where the group would meet or she had simply listened too casually when that information was passed on to her, at precisely the time the group was to convene at the hotel's east entrance, she found herself blithely examining the lobby art by the west entrance, a long city block away. Fifteen minutes later, it dawned on her that she might be in the wrong place, and she dashed the length of the hotel, arriving late, winded, and scattered.

Corbett, thoroughly enjoying his wise-old-hand-now-risen-to-great-heights role, paternalistic and very Irish, remarked—and not too quietly—to Nicole's office mate, "I see our little Nicki hasn't changed much." He undoubtedly took his companion's careful smile—after all, rookie parole officers don't argue with deputy directors—as confirmation that Nicole was still the cute little thing he thought he had known five years before. Was the stubbornness of his stereotype in part due to an age difference, since he was in his fifties and she barely thirty, or to sexist prejudices? Given his generation and background, it would be unusual if both factors didn't play a role. Prejudices are simply schemas that have been well implanted and heavily reinforced, and when they come into play, altering them becomes an even tougher task than usual.

The final bit of glue that tends to prolong old stereotypes long after they're no longer useful is a rather disagreeable but universal human trait (you can hear hints of it in any decent gossip session): we love to hear about the faults and foibles of others because they confirm our own goodness and superiority. Few things work as well to boost us out of occasional doubts and depressions as watching another's fall from grace.

In short, you're stuck with the fact that those you may be most interested in impressing will continue to see in you just what some past experience has led them to expect. If they have learned to think of you as hot tempered, immature, and not well organized, they will tend to overlook evidence that you are now a calmer, dependable person of substance, or to explain away signs of your admirable behavior as temporary aberrations or flukes.

Thankfully, the picture is not entirely gloomy. Coworkers who are constantly exposed to your behavior will at length begin to define you differently, even when the modifications in your behavioral differences have been relatively small—you now lose your temper just twice a week instead of every day, for example—as long as they continue over a long enough time. The rub is that the time required can be considerable. Studies of changes for the better in supervisory behavior have shown that it may take a year for subordinates to be convinced that the changes are real and permanent. If you would prefer not to wait that long, and particularly if those you are most anxious to impress are not working closely with you, you'll need a more concentrated approach to get them to trade in their old schema for a new, more favorable one. Although it can have many variations, your plan should include these four steps:

1. Identify what their old schemas would lead others to expect of you.

2. Do the opposite, obviously.

3. Call others' attention to the discrepancy between your behavior and what their stereotype has led them to expect.

4. Repeat the process enough times to disabuse others of the notion that your new behavior was just a fluke.

Identify What They Expect

Bothersome as it may be, you'll need to turn your mind back to the discouraging conclusions you drew from your initial efforts to ascertain just how others saw and reacted to your behavior. As disagreeable as this task feels, it will help to rein in your natural tendency to recast your old demeanor more benignly than the facts warrant. We all tend to remember past behavior in the most favorable light possible. Now characterize yourself through the eyes of those whose images you most want to change. Be ruthless. From their view, were you someone who "never really deals with poor performers," a "know-it-all who can't see shades of gray," or, like Nicole, "disorganized, immature, and emotionally unstable"? Think about what specific behaviors would follow from that perception of you. For example, if you're seen as someone who is great with people, but can't make hard decisions, at budget time anyone holding that stereotype of you would expect you to postpone or avoid difficult and unpopular cost-cutting decisions until circumstances (or more likely your boss or financial officer) make them for you.

Do the Opposite, Obviously

To break others' stereotypes of you, you must confront them with a performance that so obviously and clearly disconfirms their stereotypes that they either have to deny what they see (which is, initially, a distinct possibility) or replace their old images of you with newer, more accurate ones.

Your first step is to identify situations in which it will be practical and feasible for you to demonstrate your disconfirming behavior. Next, work out with some specificity what you're going to do and say.

For example, you have been under pressure to consolidate several departmental units under your direction, a move which would give several long-term employees an onerous choice of resigning or demoting. Your old image predicts that you will postpone such painful decisions, but the new you, though still regretful about a decision that will cause old friends distress, has faced up to its necessity. Having done your homework, you show up at next Monday's administrative meeting with a solid, fair consolidation plan. At the meeting, you interrupt the morning's proceedings to place the item on the agenda.

When your agenda item is called, you stand up to get everyone's attention; insist that putting off the decision will only prolong staff confusion; proceed to outline the reasons for your proposal; and strongly urge that the decision be confirmed before the meeting ends.

Call Others' Attention to Your Changed Behavior

After the meeting, discuss your approach to the decision with your boss, subordinates, peers, and anyone else who will listen. "It was a painful decision that had to be made fairly but quickly and decisively, and I did what I could to get us moving faster than we have in the past," you might say. Naturally, you would only say it if you meant it. Your purpose here is not to fool others into thinking that you are other than who you are, but to force them to notice the reality that the old script no longer holds.

Similarly, discuss what you've done with anyone who was present at the meeting who has been party to your developmental efforts, asking for feedback on your decisiveness (not how well you performed at the meeting). To the extent that you feel comfortable—and I would force this a little—raise the possibility that they might mention to important others the changes they've seen in you.

At times, your efforts will require more intricate plotting, planning, and the assistance of others who understand that changing your image may not occur if events are simply allowed to take their natural course. Nicole's case provides an interesting example of an image-changing plan with a larger cast of characters and a longer-term focus. It also illustrates an approach to changing the minds of senior managers with whom you have only limited contact.

When we left Nicole and Sol, they had begun to explore how to prevent her being derailed again by Dan Corbett when the next promotional opportunity opened up. Nicole's initial thought was to meet with Deputy Director Corbett and point out how successful she had become at planning and organization. Perhaps generally improving her level of acquaintance might be all that was needed.

Sol advised against this. "On the surface it sounds good, but under that hammy Irish charm, Danny's a tough old bird, and he's just as likely to see you as trying a weak-sister act. My guess is that he'd treat you to an overdose of patronizing crap. We need to surprise him, and I have an idea how we can do it."

Sol then suggested that Nicole work up a presentation for the next Probation and Parole Association meeting—he was on the program committee and could at least get her on a panel. At his suggestion, she wrote a paper describing a system she had developed for keeping tabs on the higher-risk parolees in her caseload. As Sol put it, "You won't just tell 'em you are more organized, you'll show 'em."

Nicole called Corbett, who was, in fact, a nationally known expert on community work with gangs, to check with him on the best new references for her topic, and later followed up by sending him a copy of her paper—though he hadn't asked for it—with a note thanking him for his help and hoping that he might look in on the panel discussion.

Both Sol and Nicole had earlier considered, and dismissed, the advisability of Sol traveling to headquarters to justify to Corbett why he had recommended her for promotion. Instead, Sol shared the plan he and Nicole had cooked up with his boss, Howard, the regional parole chief, and asked that he be an active participant. Although Howard was reluctant to openly challenge a higher ranking and very influential executive, he did agree to let drop whatever positive comments about Nicole might appropriately fit into the monthly executive meetings which both he and Corbett attended. As it later turned out, co-opting Howard as a fellow plotter was a wise move.

Corbett did, in fact, sit in on a portion of Nicole's presentation. Had he glanced through her paper and been impressed enough to want to see her in action? Or had he merely wanted to confirm his belief that she was immature? Or perhaps, as Nicole's paranoia whispered, he had suddenly seen her as young, attractive, and maybe naïve enough to be impressed by his own mature good looks. At any rate, he showed up, and when he strode up to the speaker's table to offer what, according to Nicole, started out as a patronizing pat on the head, she grabbed his hand, lead him around the table and introduced him to her fellow speakers, who had known him only by reputation.

Whether he was startled by Nicole's refusal to be patronized and the take-charge way she hustled him over to be introduced to her copanelists, or flattered by their respectful pleasure at meeting him, or simply impressed by her speaking presence and the quality of her performance, something jarred loose Corbett's outmoded image of her.

The first indication came that night. Seated next to Howard on the flight back from the conference, Corbett mentioned his interest in Nicole's topic and then listened in silence when Howard referred to her as the most knowledgeable and generally effective member of his parole staff. Then, as Howard later told it, without a word, Corbett turned the conversation to a reprise of some of the social highlights of the conference and his pleasure at sharing bar time with some of his old parole buddies.

Did these events radically change Corbett's opinion of Nicole? Did he now see her as an up-and-coming young star in the agency's firmament? It would be pleasant to think so, although the evidence is that something less dramatic happened. Seven months after the conference, another supervising parole officer position opened up. Once again Nicole was the prime candidate for the job, and once again her candidacy needed only confirmation by the agency director. This time, however, when the agency head raised his eyebrows to query Corbett about the proposed promotion, he merely looked bored and said, "Whatever. Can we get on with what's next on the agenda?" As Sol reported to Nicole by telephone that afternoon, "It'll take more than a changed mind to get that guy to admit that he was wrong. But, since our goal was to move him from 'no way' to neutral, I'd say we succeeded. Congratulations, kid—I mean, Ms. Supervisor."

Up till now, we've gone step by step through the general method for identifying, managing, and modifying personal attributes that have the potential to hamper your success at—and satisfaction with—your work. In Section II—"Pointers for Putting the Methods to Work"—you'll find some hints, specific suggestions, rules of thumb, and maybe some helpful perspective if your own research tells you that you need to manage one or more of the most common varieties of difficult behavior.

Section II

Pointers for Putting the Methods to Work

The next four chapters are designed to particularize the general approach covered in Chapters 1 through 5 and to help you plan your own behavior-modification program. Each chapter provides examples and specific pointers relevant to the difficult behavior patterns that I've found to be the most common targets for change. In each chapter you'll find:

- Case studies that illustrate the behavior.

- A checklist for assessing whether that variety of troublesome behavior might characterize you, at least some of the time.

- A brief list of the motivations and satisfiers commonly associated with this sort of behavior. People are complex, and the motivations and satisfactions ascribed to each variety of problem behavior may differ somewhat from your own. They are meant to be suggestive only, to orient you to the general areas in your own bundle of needs and wants that might underlie your behavior. What gives you satisfaction is important for two reasons: first, because your new, non-difficult behavior must somehow be consistent with these vital ingredients of your personality or it's unlikely that you'll stay with your program of change; and second, because those same satisfiers can function as a siren call to seduce you back into your old behavioral habits.

- Obstacles that may hinder your commitment to manage or modify your behavior.

- Situations or events that often precipitate the behavior.

- Examples of substitute behaviors that have worked for others, to get you started thinking up your own. They illustrate the need to have your substitute behaviors consistent with your own motivations, but modified enough to avoid their nonproductive effects.

- Clues that you might be slipping back to your old troublesome ways just when you thought it was all behind you.

6

Putting the Methods to Work for Hardheads, Hardnoses, and Other Potent People

Case #1: Tough-Minded Tony

Tony Leigh was one of four partners in a fast-growing computer software company. Immensely creative, he had no trouble recruiting exciting young talent into the new networks division he started. His problem was keeping them. When two of his seven initial recruits resigned before they had served the two years minimally needed for the company to benefit from the high salaries they were able to command, Tony explained, "They looked good, but they weren't what we needed. They couldn't stand the heat I was putting on them to meet our objectives."

When the third of his original "seven samurai" left soon after a shouted hallway confrontation, his partners decided they'd better dig a little deeper. They were puzzled, because with them and with their customers Tony was charming, articulate, outgoing, and exciting to be around. His subordinates, on the other hand, sketched out quite a different person. To most of them, he was a cold, sarcastic sadist who delighted in publicly humiliating them.

Rich Faro, his second in command and one of his few boosters, described a sample of his worst behavior this way: "A week ago Tony and I were reviewing Harry and Elly's new network package for our biggest airline customer, a real breakthrough for us this year. They'd allowed the schedule to slip a few weeks, but, hell, it's to be expected when you're trying for the wild blue yonder. Well, Tony just ripped into them. They hadn't told him they were behind, they weren't supervising their techs, and they didn't appreciate all the things he'd done for 'em. The worst of it is that he says all this garbage as if they were a couple of teenage punks, not the computer whizzes they are.

"When Harry and Elly left—I don't know if they were more pissed than hurt or vice versa—I told Tony he was way off base. You know what he said? Cool as anything— 'They're competent enough, Rich, but they're not *closers*. If I don't keep after them, we'll never hit our marketing goals. Besides, now they'll never slip another deadline without letting me know.'"

Tony described himself to me as tough but fair, a "complete delegator," and he did, indeed, assign out every phase of the work. However, his subordinates claimed that they had to report progress to him every week and no important actions could be taken until he had thoroughly reviewed their work and given his okay. Peculiarly enough, most of his staff—even those who found him impossible as a boss— agreed that such close follow-up might be valuable.

As Rich put it, "Tony's right, in a way. Most of the folks here are supertalented software junkies, not businesspeople. I don't think they really mind his pushing, because it helps them get their work out. I just wish that he wouldn't be so insulting. You know what Elly said to me three days after she and Harry got beat up? 'Rich, before I started to work I swore that I wouldn't let any boss make me cry, but Tony has done it twice already in the year I've been here.

High pay and challenging work or not, I don't know how long I can put up with him.'"

Case #2: Ernie, the Earnest Engineer

Ernestina Gulden worked on assignment out of a head-quarters technical-consultation group that could be tapped by any operating department that had been stumped by a knotty technical problem. In theory, consulting group staff were only to assist the field engineers, who were often reluctant to admit they needed anything more than an additional helping hand. Ernestina, however, correctly assessing that her mental equipment was superior to that of almost anyone else she might encounter, naturally assumed that her job was to survey the scene and then, having performed her mental wizardry, inform whoever had requested her consultation exactly what she, he, or they ought to do to implement her solution.

Hardest to swallow for her red-faced clients was the recognition that about 75 percent of the time her solutions to the supposedly impossible problems worked. Knowing that, but not fully understanding her modus operandi, her boss was puzzled at the steadily dropping number of requests for her services, since there were reasons to believe that the need for such services was increasing.

My interviews with regional managers and field supervisors produced no surprises:

"She's an extraordinarily smart engineer, but I can't stand the superior tone that she takes."

"She is always right, no matter how wrong she is."

"Her solutions may be technically correct, but they don't take into consideration what our customers want or how much it will cost, or what our people here can do."

"She worked on four problems for us; three of her solutions worked perfectly, and the fourth one was a disaster. My field supervisor said that he tried once to tell her that some of the parts were failing before the specs said they would, but she just got stubborn and threw her calculations in his face until he got tired of arguing. So we went ahead with her plan, and now it's taken us a year to get back to where we should have been six months ago."

"I'm still calling on Ernie when something really gets screwed up down here, because she is a very knowledgeable person, but I would sure appreciate it if she could learn to back off sometimes and leave a little room for somebody else's brain."

Tony and Ernestina were both potent forces. Not only were they personally capable, but their aggressive natures moved them into action quickly and without invitation. They influenced others into more efficient practices, and, hard hitters though they were, they earned admiration from those who recognized the value of the powerful energizing forces they could muster.

Unfortunately, the longer-term costs, both to them and to their organizations, were also very real. Because they had not learned to skillfully deploy their impulses to take charge, they left competent coworkers feeling disregarded, intimidated, and one down; they drove away others—and not just the weak and incompetent, as they had assumed—leaving little growing room for subordinates and colleagues.

While both Tony and Ernestina intimidated others, they did it differently. Tony, the hardnose, used the authority of his position and a variety of attacking behaviors to push others around. Ernie, a consummate hardhead with an overwhelming command of true expertise, employed an unshakable confidence that flowed from a conviction that she was always right, coupled with an imperviously patronizing manner.

INDICATORS THAT YOU MAY BE SEEN AS A HARDNOSE OR A HARDHEAD

You may be seen as intimidating, abrasive, or close-minded by others if

- you feel surrounded by wimps and yes-people who never stand up to you (you're a hardnose) or by sloppy incompetents who have never heard of thoroughness and follow-through (you're a hardhead)

- your boss has suggested that you learn to communicate better, listen more, or be friendlier

- it has been suggested that you are a black-and-white thinker who has trouble seeing shades of gray

- you've been mistakenly accused of being stubborn, rigid, or dogmatic, even though you know that you're just a confident, strong-minded individual who perseveres in the face of doubt

- you often feel a secret rush when others meekly or resentfully do what you tell them, especially when they don't want to do it

- you can't help feeling superior to those who don't stand up to your vigorous manner or your well-marshaled facts and logic

MOTIVATIONS AND SEDUCTIVE SATISFIERS THAT OFTEN UNDERLIE THIS BEHAVIOR

Motivations

- a strong and deep-seated need to take charge, strongly influence, or control your environment by controlling others (You're a hardnose.)

- a strong need to predict and control your environment by using information, logic, and rationality, and by demonstrating that your version of reality is the only one (You're a hardhead.)

Seductive Satisfiers

- seeing others scurrying to implement your ideas, plans, and orders

- proving once again that you are superior, competent, and strong compared to others

- feeling competent and in control of problems and people

OBSTACLES TO YOUR COMMITMENT TO MANAGE THE BEHAVIOR

- the difficulty in acknowledging a continuing temptation to confirm your own invulnerability by exposing the weaknesses of others (It does feel good to feel powerful and omniscient.)

PRECIPITATING FACTORS THAT MAY EVOKE THE BEHAVIOR

- another's tone of voice, stance, or choice of words perceived as a challenge to your authority or your ability to maintain control

- disagreement with your idea, instruction, or plan

- whining, complaining, placating, or other signs of weakness in others

- a slipped deadline or a need to rush a project through

SUBSTITUTE BEHAVIORS

- When a problem is brought to your attention, require of yourself that you *always* follow this prime directive of interpersonal effectiveness (I call it Rule #1): Listen first before correcting, blaming, giving orders, or pushing your plan.

- Use alternate, less demeaning language for forcefully presenting your thoughts. For example:

  —"I need to insist," instead of, "Do it!" (For reasons not entirely clear to me, the former seems to have less sting than the latter.)
  —"Do you want to add anything to the plan before you move on it?" instead of, "Just do it my way."

- When you realize you have slipped and are again running over a coworker's objections or hesitation, say, "Wait a minute, Rich, tell me again what *you* would do."

- When you realize you have been buffaloing a coworker or customer with your superior logic, try, "I think my facts are right, but maybe I've missed the real point you're making. Please say it again."

- To reduce the personal-attack quality of a sarcastic remark, say, "I was sarcastic just now because I really think this is important."

- When you realize you've given others their marching orders in too sharp a manner ("What are you waiting for? Go!"), say, "I know I sound short, but I'm anxious for us to get moving. We'll talk more about it later."

- When you are aware that your vigorously stated opinion has been interpreted as a decision, thereby precluding a useful discussion, insert, "That's where I am right now; it's not a decision."

Clues That You Might Be Slipping

- Your fingers are pointing directly at another or jabbing his shoulder as you speak.

- You feel irritated and impatient as you bark out orders.

- Your voice has an edge, or you sound sarcastic: "Are you *finally* ready to get on with it?"

- You realize that you've begun lecturing a coworker rather than engaging in a discussion.

Keep in Mind

Surprisingly, I have found that hard cases like you have the best prognosis for modifying your behavior, although your subordinates will not believe it possible until they see that it is a lasting change. I mention this because if you do tend toward the contentious end of the continuum, your first step is a giant one, and you're likely to find it irksome. Feeling potent when you have prevailed over your less aggressive fellows is fun, and regularly reminding yourself how much it is limiting your opportunities is a bore. But that is the necessary first step.

Specifically, as soon as possible after you've yelled at, steam-rollered, or cut down a favored victim, you'll need to force upon yourself a moment's reflection. During those few seconds of thought, remind yourself that others may see you less as a top gun and more as an unpromotable brawler or a stubborn know-it-all who lacks interpersonal skills, a likely handicap in these litigious times of sensitive-knowledge workers, generational value differences, and other changes in the nature of the workplace.

There is good evidence that quiet reflection just after a behavioral slip—not really your strong point, perhaps, but try it anyway—facilitates learning and retaining useful interpersonal skills for those whose transgressions are of an aggressive nature. If you do it enough, you'll finally be able to profit from the people-oriented training programs that you formerly avoided or sat through with bored resistance. Best of all, you'll have the satisfaction of knowing that you're having an easier time of managing your difficult behavior than those whose troublesome qualities are being less outgoing and uninhibited.

7

Putting the Methods to Work When You're Too Nice, Too Helpful, or Too Caring

THE BEHAVIOR

Case #1: Friendly Frieda

At first it was hard for me to see why Frieda Bassett, the lone safety consultant in an insurance company regional office, was concerned about her future, because everyone at every level seemed happy to have her around. At thirty-eight, she looked and acted ten years younger, seemed always in a good humor, regularly defused potential conflicts with gentle witticisms, and was the mainstay of the office Pizza and Party Society, which made sure that birthdays and promotions were well celebrated.

At our initial meeting—it was over lunch, at her insistence—she took the lead with perky chatter, asked questions about the training and team building that were part of my consultation to the company, and listened to my answers with wide-eyed admiration.

Midway through our lunch, I reminded her that she had

mentioned a problem she wanted to discuss. It was as if an invisible hand had stripped her face of any feeling. "The fact is," she said, "I've been everyone's friend for twelve years, and I've had exactly one promotion—from safety rep to safety consultant—to show for it. My stats are good; I've shown I'm good with people; so why haven't I been made a manager?"

"What does Jack"—the regional manager—"say?" I asked.

"That's exactly why I'm here," she said. "When I asked him that, he said that I'm a great person and he's lucky to have me on his staff, but I don't have enough *substance* to be a manager. What the hell does that mean?"

The next day I asked Jack about Frieda. "Yeah," he said thoughtfully, "I mentioned that she might want to talk with you about it, since she couldn't seem to get what I was trying to tell her. But it's not an easy thing to explain. How can I say, 'Frieda, you're just too enthusiastic, too friendly, too cheerful, and absolutely too accommodating'? Besides, it's more than that. She never disagrees with anyone, including me. I don't mean she always *does* what I want, but she never confronts me openly. I can't in good conscience recommend her as a manager or to be trained for a senior staff job. It's really too bad, because she's such a heck of a nice person."

Case #2: Idealist Ilene

Ilene Sowers sold high-ticket high-tech electronic instruments. Her success rate was the highest in the company, but her particular point of pride was that more and more customers were turning away from their previous suppliers to order from her. Her secret, she said, was that she listened and generally poked around until she understood the problems facing her customers. Then she proposed solutions to those problems, often at a lower cost than they had anticipated, and even, at times, suggested that they try out a cheaper competing product to see if it might do. How could they not be convinced that both she and her company could be trusted to follow through with service and technical support?

So why were her boss and her boss's boss not only disappointed in her performance but also considering transferring her to a much less leveraged and less profitable line? Because Ilene repeatedly, in the face of direct orders to the contrary, negotiated (her bosses referred to it as "giving away") huge discounts and exorbitant warranty terms.

"Our long-term future depends on loyal customers, not squeezing high profits out of this current product," Ilene told me. "Besides, most of our customers are in the health business one way or another, and they're being bled from every direction. I know they're hurting and can't afford the prices we're asking."

"Sure, there's something to what Ilene's told you," said her boss, "and we know that. But I had that territory before her, and I heard those same old poor-mouthing stories for years. Yeah, hospitals are having it tougher now, but it's also true that Ilene's a sucker for a sob story, and those hospital administrative types know just how to play her."

Case #3: Carl, the Closet Codependent

Of Carl Milner's seven direct reports, only two—the most competent two—had anything negative to say. Both evaluators started off in the same positive vein as the others. Carl, they assured me, was a warm, supportive, knowledgeable, and ethical boss. But unlike their fellow agents, they also pointed to a less noble side.

"Carl is a wonderful person," said one. "He really cares, not only about the goals of the agency, but about the people in his regional office. But what bugs me, and I've told him this, is the way he has let some people get away with half-assed work for years. And of course the rest of us have to pick up the slack."

His equally critical coworker was even more specific: "Carl will ask Jim (another agent) for an interim report by Friday, knowing that it will have to be at headquarters by, say, Monday or Tuesday. On Friday, Jim, who's ass I'd have canned years ago, will give him a sketchy draft, if that, and Daddy Carl will take it home, completely rewrite it over the weekend, and then send it off over Jim's signature. Carl loses a weekend—and I know that really bothers him, because he's a family man—while that fuck-off Jim gets credit for a fine report. Every once in a while, Carl will lose it with Jim—yell at him and slam out of his office. But sure enough, two hours later he's back apologizing to Jim for losing his cool. How do I know? Because Jim and I share an office. If there's such a thing as being too nice and too caring, Carl's surely it."

Yes, there is such a thing as being too nice, too accommodating, and too friendly, but if you're a Frieda, Ilene, or Carl, it's not always easy to know when you've crossed the line. After all, don't most people hope to be liked or at least accepted? Don't they sympathize with others' distress and offer a helping hand to those in trouble? And shouldn't they?

Surely, but when you do not balance these impulses with an equal willingness to set boundaries and insist that others live up to agreements they have made, such undoubted virtues can rob you of power and effectiveness. Certainly, a tendency toward being overly helpful or accommodating can burden any relationship, but it is particularly dissonant when you control scarce resources for which others compete—promotions, pay raises, plum assignments—because you'll invariably displease or disappoint someone. In doing so, you risk the loss of their regard or must endure the pain of sympathetically sharing their distress.

Realistically, you are not likely to become less sensitive to others' anguish or less interested in their friendship. But you may gain the resolution to do what you must by reminding yourself that it is at length a cruel sort of kindness to help others avoid the consequences of their acts. Or, if your niceness is more in the ever-eager style of superagreeable Frieda, remember that while an adeptness at flattery *will* often get you anywhere with most people, reality is better served by honest appraisal and constructive disagreement.

INDICATORS THAT YOU MAY HAVE CROSSED THE LINE

Others may see you as someone who is "a very nice (helpful, caring, friendly) person" but "indecisive," "a soft touch," "not a leader," "not tough enough for the job" if

- You have noticed that while you make small decisions easily ("Postpone the meeting until Tuesday."), you tend to procrastinate on or dodge those that are consequential, especially if they involve choosing among rivals. For example, you schedule interminable interviews with outside candidates to avoid selecting from a stable of several advancement-hungry subordinates, equally eager for promotion.

- You find yourself frequently consummating deals that are only marginally profitable for yourself or your organization.

- You notice that you consistently convey an impression that you agree with or support a coworker's position or product, in spite of inner doubts and reservations.

- You much prefer conflict-free relationships and don't understand why others seem to relish an escalating argument.

- You frequently find yourself trying to appease or avoid others who disagree or are in conflict, rather than weathering the adversarial atmosphere and staying focused on solving the problem at hand.

- You often do pick-up work, both literally, by disposing of dirty coffee cups after a meeting, and figuratively, by redoing others' incompetent or sloppy work to make it right, often without taking credit for your contribution (although you may secretly hope that they will show appreciation).

- You feel resentful at having to work harder to make up for others' poor performance, but you seldom express that resentment directly to the guilty parties. Occasionally, you may lose your temper and accuse them of wrongdoing, but you usually try to make amends for this improper outburst by apologizing or ignoring the next round of troublesome behavior.

- You find yourself repeatedly trying to improve others by lecturing, coaxing, or nagging at them. You may or may not see the difference between this method of developing others and the alternative of clearly stating both expectations and consequences and allowing the consequences to do the developing.

- You often feel trapped between the refusal of others to change for the better and your own discomfort at the thought of taking any disciplinary action that would distress you because it distresses them.

MOTIVATIONS AND SEDUCTIVE SATISFACTIONS THAT OFTEN UNDERLIE THIS BEHAVIOR

Motivations

- You were saddled very early in life with those never-to-be-questioned parental injunctions that come under the heading of "Rules For Proper Living": Always be nice, never cause hurt, happily share, and invariably be helpful to others.

- You probably also have a healthier dose of altruism than most. It is a motivation of which the world has much need, but like any potential for good, it can be misapplied.

Seductive Satisfactions

- That warm glow when those you've helped show appreciation. Although they may seldom be so forthcoming, the rarity of the event magnifies the effect.

- The solid feeling of accomplishment when you've provided quality service to others or you've acted in an ethical, caring way.

POTENTIAL OBSTACLES TO YOUR COMMITMENT TO MANAGE THE BEHAVIOR

- Because you are such an agreeable person, others may find it particularly difficult to be candid with you about the troublesome aspects of your behavior.

- In any single instance, it will never be completely clear whether you are extending a usefully helping hand or an indulgent pat on the head. You'll need to keep an eye on the pattern: Are you almost always the one who repairs the inadequate work of others? Do you usually avoid stressful interactions?

- It will be tempting to explain away each codependent incident or adroit sidestepping as an essential part of your peaceable nature ("I just don't like hassles."). You thus avoid facing the additive effect of too much niceness.

- Because you know that you are often quite vociferous and willing to take a stand about the unethical or inconsiderate actions of organizations, institutions, and high-ranking officials, you may dismiss the allegations of others that you are too nice, which they have based upon your seeming unwillingness to deal with the incompetence or irresponsibility of subordinates or teammates.

PITFALLS AND PRECIPITATING EVENTS THAT MAY EVOKE THE BEHAVIOR

- You see the "I really want it" look on the face of someone who is importuning you to decide in her favor. For example, a salesperson who seems both sincere and needful wants a big order from you. While there are other demands on your budget, you *could* squeeze out a sizable order.

- You pick up clues that others may not like you. For example, the training class you are leading shows signs of boredom while you are lecturing.

- You feel unappreciated. For example, you help out a coworker who seemed swamped, only to have your contribution ignored, patronized, or unfairly criticized.

Examples of Substitute Behaviors

These substitute behaviors were designed to set necessary limits, and yet be consonant with impulses to be supportive and accommodating to others.

- "I can see how much you want me to say yes, but to do my job well I have to say no."

- In response to pressure to change your mind after you have made a considered decision and explained why, say, "It's just not possible." If asked, "Why not?" respond with, "Sorry, it's just not possible." If pushed still further, say, "We'll discuss it later, if it's important." (The time for discussion is before the decision has been made. Since most decisions result from weighing a complexity of trade-offs, there will always be counterarguments for any of your reasons. Only a need for action ever ends that sort of debate.)

- "My job requires that I make judgments about how well members of my staff are performing. By the standards we've agreed on, you're not doing very well."

- "On the one hand, I feel sympathetic about how the recession has hurt your business, but on the other hand, I have to keep my own business sound. Your product is just not what we need right now (is one we've had repair problems with, doesn't have the quality we need)."

- When you feel yourself acceding to decisions about which you still have doubts, say, "I need some time alone to consider this. I'll call you in a hour (this afternoon, next Monday)."

- When you hear yourself make an overly optimistic promise ("I'll have it ready by Wednesday."), say, "Hold on, I'd better check the schedule." Pause while you smile at the persistence of that impulse to please, and confirm a more realistic deadline, saying, "I'd better make that Friday to be sure."

- When you are required to deal with disagreement or conflict, say, "In my experience, there's usually at least some aspects that are right on both sides . . ."

CLUES THAT YOU MIGHT BE SLIPPING

- You are not yet fully convinced, yet you hear yourself say, "If you really want to, I guess it's okay."

- You feel so guilty when you start to inform staff members of their poor performance that you find yourself unable to talk to them the way you've talked *about* them to your boss or thought about them to yourself.

- When someone looks or sounds disapproving—a customer doesn't return your smile, for example—you find yourself frantically trying to please him. You joke around rather than continuing on with your carefully planned demonstration or sales presentation.

- You find yourself resentfully ruminating about coworkers who seem to slack off because they know that you'll always pitch in to get the work done.

KEEP IN MIND

Your strengths are your ability to feel for and with others and your understanding of how relationships are the key to organizational effectiveness. Capitalize on those potent forces, but curb their overuse by coupling sensitivity ("I can see how much you want me to say yes . . .") with the limits imposed by reality and responsibility ("but my job calls for me to say no"). Buttress yourself with the knowledge that judiciously applied boundaries foster growth, a fact to which any good nursery person, pruning shears in hand, will cheerfully attest.

8

Putting the Methods to Work When You've Been Accused of Complaining or Negativism

THE BEHAVIOR

Case #1: Cathy, the Competent Complainer

"What do you do, Dr. B," wailed City Manager Dick Olsen, "when you have an administrative assistant who is a joy to look at, superefficient, good at handling the public, and a constant complainer? I hardly have my coat off in the morning before Cathy starts in on Paul (assistant city manager), who hasn't come in yet, or maybe it was that he left at four thirty the day before. Then it's the mayor's office that's undermining our authority, or the Public Works Department that's browbeating the citizens, the secretarial pool that's poorly run, and finally, do I realize I haven't done my expense report for last month?

"I don't just shut her up, partly because she seems so well meaning and partly because I think maybe it's stuff I ought to be paying attention to. And Cathy's not so easy to stop. When I asked her to take the office problems to Paul, she just nodded her head and said that she only tells me what I ought to know. Right now it's all I can do to be polite and pretend to listen.

"Last night, when I was fighting my way through the commuter traffic, I kept thinking that if I have to sit through her self-righteous, faultfinding little lectures one more time I'll lose it and say some things I won't be able to take back.

"Why haven't I fired her? Because in every other way, she's just the kind of person I need to do this crazy job. She keeps me organized, and a couple of times she's saved my ass when I was moving too fast without facts to back me up. And of course, can you really fire someone whose only fault is that she constantly nags and complains? Probably not. But if a good reason for reclassifying her position downward came up, I might just do it. And in these days of shrinking budgets, Doc, that might be sooner rather than later."

Case #2: Ned, a Never-Any-Pie-in-the-Sky Negativist

It was a perfect setting for bright hopes—a rustic resort redolent of easy comfort in a pine-forested valley, complete with the mirror stillness of a mountain lake. Everyone's mood—well, the mood of almost everyone—was exuberant. The conferees, all members of the state Health and Welfare Department, were optimistic about finding solutions to long-standing problems. Wasn't there a new, more politically favored governor and a high probability of tapping into the federal money machine?

It didn't take long, however—say, fifteen minutes—for those thirteen dedicated people to see how illusory their optimism had been. They'd been skillfully guided to that deflating realization by Ned Wilshire. The dialogue went like this:

ANN ELLEN (leader of the group): Our toughest problem is quality foster homes. Let's start with that.

FRED (superintendent of a camp for troubled youngsters): I agree, but the answer's simple—we need a better per diem for the foster parents. With the present cap on what we can pay them, all we get are the dregs or a few good people who have to take on too many kids just to make ends meet.

NED: We might as well quit, then. We'll never get the bureaucrats who head this department to give us the foster-parent rate we need.

PHYLLIS (a unit supervisor): That's been true in the past, Ned, but now—

NED (interrupting): Nothing's really changed, and you know it, Phyll. The new governor is as political as the old one. They're only interested in votes, and kids without families don't vote, and their parents—if they have them—don't vote, either. And even if we got some more money in the foster parents' fund, the department brass would never let us raise the rates we can pay. What they *would* do is push us to get more crummy homes instead of upgrading the ones we have now, because it would make the numbers look better.

ANN ELLEN (dismayed and trying to get the meeting back on track): The point is, how should we go about presenting what we need so it will get attention?

NED: Ann Ellen, why do you persist in this exercise in futility? When have we ever gotten any real attention from the director of this agency? He's been around forever because he knows how to kiss up to whoever's in the statehouse. He doesn't care about foster kids or any other kind of kids. What happened the last time you put in a raised budget request?

ANN ELLEN: Well, I'll admit it didn't go anywhere then, but . . .

NED (looking around triumphantly): See? This whole conference is just a ploy to make us feel like they're paying attention. They're not.

ANN ELLEN (desperately): Shall we try the next problem on our agenda?

DON (another conferee): Well, what I really want to know is who's up for a round of golf when we're through here? Look at what a beautiful day it is. Why don't we finish up tonight—those who want to, I mean?

Both complainers and negativists have important things to say. But the ironic fate of complainers is that the manner in which they point up the failings and blunders of their fellows insures that neither they nor their reports of wrongdoing will be taken seriously. Negativists have the opposite problem: genuinely disheartened, they superbly articulate the dark side and erode the enthusiasm and determination that just might have prevailed over seemingly insurmountable obstacles. Therefore, the goal of both complainers and negativists is to learn how to express their concerns as problems rather than pronouncements.

YOU MAY BE SEEN AS A COMPLAINER OR NEGATIVIST IF . . .

- you repeatedly report coworkers' failings to your boss or to other coworkers

- your boss or coworkers often show signs of restlessness or inattention when you are raising problems or issues

- you have been jokingly praised, or you have praised yourself, for always taking the devil's advocate position

- upon paying attention, you notice a whining, nagging, or singsong quality to your voice when you are commenting on the behavior of others

- upon paying attention, you notice that your words and manner often imply that you are being unfairly treated

- you often feel impatient and annoyed with others who seem oblivious to the incompetence, irresponsibility, and even evil that seems so plain to you

- you are usually the one who points out the negative aspects of a competent or otherwise enjoyable performance

MOTIVATIONS AND SEDUCTIVE SATISFIERS THAT OFTEN UNDERLIE THIS BEHAVIOR

Motivations

- a view of the world that emphasizes how imperfect most things are

- an accompanying sense of near hopelessness that the model world you envision can ever be achieved

- distrust that those with power and authority will behave responsibly

- extreme discomfort when others do not behave as you believe they should

Seductive Satisfactions

- a wonderful feeling of being courageously in the right when you have accurately blamed those who are behaving improperly or unwisely or when you have called to task those in authority who have not yet taken corrective action

- that sense of completeness and personal affirmation when events have proved that your more pessimistic view was accurate

- the virtuous feeling that percolates through a discussion of who is to blame

Obstacles to Your Commitment to Manage the Behavior

- You find yourself unwilling or unable to question the belief that unless success is assured, problem solving is a fruitless endeavor.

- You can't quite grasp the distinction between a *complaint,* the statement of a problem ("The lack of private interviewing rooms interferes with obtaining confidential information."), and *complaining,* which is passively blaming someone for a misdeed ("Why can't we ever have the kind of interviewing space we need?").

Pitfalls and Precipitating Events That May Evoke the Behavior

- Political or organizational changes leave you feeling less control over your life. Examples:

—An expanded workload now requires that work that was solely yours must be shared with others.

—You feel disenfranchised because political figures you supported lose out in local, state, or national elections.

—Your organizational entity is swallowed in a merger or acquisition.

- Issues and problems that you have brought to your boss's attention are dismissed or ignored.

Substitute Behaviors

- When you believe that you may have slipped into a complaining model, say, "I may sound like I'm just complaining, but I believe we have some real problems to solve. Let me restate them."

- When you realize you have been throwing cold water on everyone's proposed solutions, assert, "I realize I sound negative, but I'm just trying to point out the pitfalls we'll have to be careful of."

- "If I sound like I'm blaming you for everything, I don't mean to. It's just that I can see your part in it better than I can see mine. You can help me with that."

- To your boss or a coworker with whom you work closely, suggest, "Look, if I ever sound like I'm just whining and complaining at you, just ask, 'What do you need?'"

- When you feel concerned about what's happening but helpless to change it, try to identify one small step that you can take that might have even a minor effect. For example, others in your unit consistently come in late, increasing your own early-morning workload. Rather than complaining, write a note to your boss (signed or unsigned) suggesting that expectations about when the work day begins, and the consequences of irregular hours, be discussed at the next staff meeting.

CLUES THAT YOU MAY BE SLIPPING BACK INTO COMPLAINING OR NEGATIVISM

- Your problem formulations begin to sound like a litany of "who's to blame."

- You hear yourself stating contingencies ("The brass may not listen") as if they were pronouncements of reality ("They'll never listen to us!").

KEEP IN MIND

Optimists often succeed by cheerfully blinding themselves to very real impediments that might discourage them from trying. Small wonder that they are irritated by carping and gloomy pronouncements and enervated by the parade of nasty truths that they would have much preferred to ignore. So if you are one of those who doesn't always take the rosy view and who tries to tell those pie-in-the-sky optimists what's what, you shouldn't be surprised when they resentfully call you a complainer or a negativist and try to stay out of your way. Worse, the way you have communicated the realities that you clearly see—and they try not to—interferes with their realizing that your glass-is-half-empty view is actually a perfect complement to their overoptimism.

So the essence of your behavior-modification efforts will be to attend more to *how* you say it than to *what* you say. First, you'll need to cast your litany of errors, faults, and obstacles as problems or contingencies that might possibly be resolved or avoided, rather than as immutable blockages. The second requirement, often the most difficult for my complaining clients, is to *describe* the consequences that accrue from what's not working well, rather than who's to blame for it. When Cathy learned to say, "When both you and Paul don't come in until nine, I'm forced to lie when the mayor calls," rather than, "Paul is always late," she got action from Dick, not anger.

9

Putting the Methods to Work When You're Touchy, Terrible-Tempered, or Tearful

THE BEHAVIOR

Case #1: Terrible-Tempered Ted

Middle age had softened Ted Cosel's profile and added about twenty pounds of excess weight to his six feet of brawn, but he was still an imposing physical force. I had thought he might be reluctant to meet with me—the referral had come from the plant manager at the instigation of the shop steward—so it was a pleasant surprise when he welcomed me into his plain-as-a-nail office, plied me with coffee, and set about setting me straight.

I interrupted what sounded like the beginning of a recital of his accomplishments to say, "You know, both Joe and Harvey are absolutely in your corner. What they told me was that you are the best materials manager anyone ever had, except that sometimes you blow your stack. Now you've done it one time too many, and it's gone before the union grievance committee. What's all this about you punishing a crew by not letting them eat lunch?"

"Now wait a damn minute, I never . . ." Ted began. Then he sat back, grimaced once, and described himself to me this way: "It's true that I have a temper, Dr. Bramson. I've always had a low flash point. I mean, I get angry about things that other people seem to pass off. But that's the way I am. I know that Joe has sicced you on me because he doesn't want any union problems, but I think he's exaggerating how bad it really is. Anyway, I can't believe that holding my feelings in is a good thing to do. As a psychologist you must agree with that."

"Tell me about the last time you lost it," I said.

"Okay, it was three days ago at noon. A big shipment of specialty metals from one of our vendors was due, and there was no one to be seen on the loading dock. I took the call from the lead driver, who said he was about ten miles out and would arrive in twenty minutes or so. I found James (one of the warehouse foremen) and three of his boys hanging out in the coffee room, where there's no phone. I chewed out James for not covering the office, then made them finish their lunches out on the dock. Yeah, I know it was not the guys' fault and they should have had their full half hour for lunch, and maybe I was too hard on James."

"Did you listen to his side of it before you lit into him?" I asked.

"Well, no. I suppose I should have, but it's his job to see that every in and out shipment is handled right. The phone should not have been left uncovered."

"Well," I said, "it looks like he made a mistake. But was it a big one, worth getting dumped on, a small one, worth a reminder, or somewhere in between?"

"There *is* an answering machine," said Ted, thoughtfully, "so if he intended to check it in time to get set up for the shipment, I guess it wasn't such a huge mistake. So I shouldn't have lost my temper. It's not that I haven't tried— Joe's not the first one to pull my chain about my getting angry too much—but then the next thing I know someone screws up and I get sore. Now if you have any magic for me, I'd like to hear it."

"Well," I said, "sounds to me as if instead of trying to not get angry, which obviously hasn't worked, you ought to get better at being irritated and annoyed. Then when someone screws up a little, you won't be stuck with either giving them both barrels or ignoring it."

"You mean you want me to stop and think about *how* angry I should be and not *whether* I should be angry. Well, that might be interesting to try."

Case #2: Sensitive Sunny, Tough and Tearful

Sunny Matthews had left word with the CEO's secretary that she wanted an appointment with me on my next consulting visit. I knew she was one of the corporate-level Human Resources managers who reported directly to the H.R. vice president, but our acquaintance had never moved beyond head-nodding in the hall.

"Dr. Bramson," she said before either of us had settled into our chairs, "I am a crier—have been since I was a child. No problem when I'm at home or with friends—they all know it's just the way I am—but at work it's the world's greatest nuisance. Whenever one of the men I deal with begins to get offensive—you know, implying that I'm stupid or being bureaucratic or something like that—I can feel the tears starting. Mostly I can control it and keep on making my points, but sometimes it just gets away from me. The tears come, my voice gets choked up, and the meeting stops in its tracks.

"Some of the men just seem embarrassed and look away, and a few are just openly angry. I suppose they think I'm using the tears to make them go along with what I want. It's worse when they get solicitous—do I want a glass of water? I've taken to just saying, 'I'll get back to you,' and walking out. Lord knows what they say when I'm gone."

"How are you feeling just before the tears start to come?" I asked.

"Usually hurt and angry all mixed together. Mostly angry. But once I feel like I might cry—you know, that pressure behind the eyeballs—I feel absolutely inadequate, a sissy girl being picked on by the big kids. The crazy part is that most of the time I come across as a very decisive person who is willing to take a tough stand on important issues."

She was now openly crying, tears streaming, voice raspy. "But, geez, look at me now, thirty-eight years old, starting to get gray, and bawling. Absolutely not vice-presidential material."

"Well," I said, "I'd say you have two problems and one fun task: how to do something other than cry when you're hurt and angry, how to get over being angry at yourself because you cry instead of pounding the table, and teaching the guys you work most closely with that when you *do* cry it means you're too angry for words and you'll shortly tell them why."

Stormy behavior—glaring eyes, hostile gestures, bitter, accusing words—and crying are the raw unthinking defensive behaviors we examined in Chapter 3. Your most primitive defenses are roused because you suspect that someone or something threatens your cherished plans or some other important part of your self. True, crying is more versatile than rage, because it may accompany any intense feeling—joy, sadness, and even patriotic fervor—but the tears that are the most troublesome at work are those that follow from your belief that your personal worth is under attack.

Like all defensive maneuvers, angry raging and tears work by provoking dismay, stupefied silence, concern, or pity, alone or in combination. The net effect is that your opposition is derailed or at least sidetracked. So it's not hard to see why these protective behaviors reinforce themselves, which makes them hard to give up and perhaps seduces you into excusing them as "just the way I am." Luckily, you also have the capacity to act as if you were not that way.

Defensive responses like these may often seem torn from you unexpectedly and with such little warning that preventing them may not be possible much of the time. So your task will be threefold: first, to invent ways to stop the behavior before it gets out of hand; second, to sensitize yourself to any behavioral and feeling cues that may precede an episode of temper or tears; and third, to try to identify, and then reframe, those perspectives that underlie your tendency to overreact. Ted Cosel did, at length, realize that not all screwups were awful and that he could tell the difference between those that deserved an "oops" and those worthy of a bit of well-placed temper.

YOU MAY BE SEEN AS TOUCHY IF . . .

- more than occasionally you angrily say things you later regret

- from time to time you feel so overwhelmed with anger that you express it physically, by throwing something, for example, slamming a document down, shoving a book off a table, or striking the table with your fist

- you periodically apologize to subordinates or coworkers for losing your cool

- you have been chided—perhaps with a smile—about your Irish (or other ethnic) temper

- you've been called moody or overemotional

- discussions at meetings you conduct are guarded, and there is little staff participation, even though you have asked for it

- you sometimes avoid entering into or continuing on with an important discussion because you are concerned that if you do, you may cry

- in the past your peers have occasionally aborted a conflict-producing but important discussion because you showed signs of being emotionally overwhelmed

MOTIVATIONS AND SEDUCTIVE SATISFIERS THAT OFTEN UNDERLIE THE BEHAVIOR

Motivations

- strong inner drives to reach your goals quickly so that you often have less tolerance than others for obstacles and frustrations

- early-learned beliefs (of which of you may be only partly aware) that anyone who blocks you, threatens your values, or doesn't behave as he or she should is a bad person who deserves to be attacked and punished

Seductive Satisfiers

- the bittersweet feeling of exhausted release after an outburst (bitter because you also feel guilty about your loss of control)

- secret satisfaction that your opposition or "enemies" have been stumped (even though you are somewhat aware that your method also has costs for yourself)

Obstacles to Your Commitment to Manage the Behavior

- a belief that withholding the direct expression of strong feelings will have undesirable effects on your physical or mental health

- a belief that behavior that is driven by strong emotions cannot be controlled

Pitfalls and Precipitating Events That May Evoke the Behavior

- You feel blocked or frustrated in pursuit of your goals (for example, at 5 P.M. you discover typos in an important letter you were intending to send out today).

- From others' words, postures, gestures, or facial expressions you infer that you or your work are under attack (for example, just as you finish explaining your idea, you see a rival for available resources nudge and whisper to the coworker sitting next to him).

- Others violate your sense of fair play or proper behavior (for example, you hear that a friend had lunch with a coworker who—and your friend surely knew it—has been telling lies about you).

- Your work is challenged in the area in which you are most unsure of your knowledge or competence.

SUBSTITUTE BEHAVIORS

To Manage Crying

- Discover or invent, and then practice, nonverbal signals that inform others that you need time to think. Examples are the palm-out "halt" sign, the time-out signal used in many sports, and tilting your head downward or facing up toward the ceiling, eyes closed, both palms out.

- Adopt a habit of periodically shading your eyes with your hands, turning to face a wall, and so forth, when thinking hard. Perform this act frequently enough so that it is accepted as something you do when you're thinking, rather than as a mask for tear-filled eyes. If you have qualms about such role playing, remind yourself that you are not concealing your spontaneous reaction because it is reprehensible but because it interferes with your ability to deal effectively with others and may send signals you do not intend (that is, "take care of me").

- If tears have already started, say, "Don't let my tears stop you. I cry when I'm angry (annoyed, irritated, frustrated), and I want to keep going."

- When you first begin to feel the angry hurt that often precedes tears say, "I need a short break for some coffee (to go to the rest room, get some papers). How about taking five?" Or simply signal time-out, lift your cup, and head for the coffee or the rest room.

To Manage Angry Outbursts

- When you feel like yelling, scolding, or lecturing, close your mouth tightly, sit down, and stay silent for ten seconds (count them to yourself—an old but effective device).

- Distract yourself by searching for something in your brief-case or pocket, pouring coffee, and so forth.

- Force a break in the interaction by going to the rest room, asking for a coffee break, and the like.

- When back in control, state, as calmly as you can, "Tell me again what you're trying to accomplish (what your goal is)."

- To avoid misinterpreting another's words or behavior, ask, "You smiled (frowned, winked, rolled your eyes) when I made my last point. What was your thought?"

- When you realize you've been raging because you feel blocked, say, "I obviously have a lot of feelings about this. Tell me again why you think we should not go ahead."

- As a follow-up to an outburst, instead of apologizing, say, "My temper really got away from me yesterday. Yelling at people is not what I want to do, because it certainly gets in the way and no one likes to be yelled at. Part of what set me off was the unexpected delay in our getting those replacement parts. What can we do to prevent that in the future?"

To Modify Your Tendencies to Cry or Lose Your Temper

- Use mental rehearsal (review the relevant sections in Chapter 4) to give you confidence in using the braking maneuvers and other substitute behaviors.

- Assume that it is your *interpretation* of a provoking situation and the motives of those involved that make you hurt or angry, not the situation itself. For example, when you are privately debriefing a raging or crying episode, ask yourself, "Why was I so overwhelmingly angry, rather than simply annoyed, irritated, or amused by what the others did or said?" Your thoughts might go something like this: "It makes sense that I'd be irritated with Shirley when she quipped about all the detail in my proposal, but it wasn't a horrible disaster. So what was I thinking about her that made it seem as if she had committed a crime?"

At the very least, you'll become more familiar with the kinds of interpretations that tend to provoke your temper or your tears. Over time, you'll be less surprised by your reaction and better able to cope. But there is the even more helpful possibility that you may discover some inner beliefs (that you weren't really aware you had) that are, at least in part, sheer nonsense. It's not always easy to uncover these notions, because they're usually "truths" that you've always known to be so.

For example, a bundle of inner beliefs that was a first-class provoker of both tears and temper in a senior staff manager (who later did become a vice president) was: "A really competent person is always confident and sure of anything she does. Therefore, if anyone can point out errors or weak areas in my proposal, I must be inadequate and no good [tears], and anyone who criticizes me is terrible and deserves to be punished and hurt [scathing personal attack]."

While a full-scale examination of such unrealistic beliefs without the aid of a counselor or therapist (more about this in the next chapter) may be more of a task than you're yet ready for, I've found that even the barest glimpse of the nature of these beliefs makes the full use of substitute behaviors much easier.

SIGNS THAT YOU MAY BE SLIPPING

- You hear yourself justifying a temper loss as okay because you were provoked by someone's poor behavior.

- You find yourself accepting favors from those who are either genuinely moved by or afraid of provoking your tears.

- Your outbursts continue, but you feel inner resistance to working out your own substitute behaviors, mentally rehearsing them, or identifying the factors that precipitate your behavior.

KEEP IN MIND

The most devastating effects of your fight-or-flight reactions will be most acutely felt by those over whom you have power. Naturally, the best way to mitigate those effects is also the least comfortable—openly acknowledge that you now realize that you can sometimes be a pain and that you intend to find a better way to express your feelings.

The most rapid progress in managing touchy behavior I've ever seen was demonstrated by an executive who gave his staff— including his secretary—permission to leave the room whenever he sounded as if he was escalating into the irate, nasty carping that had earned him the epithet "old sour ball." After some hesitation they agreed to honor his request—if he would put it in writing. He did, and they did.

The results were dramatic. As he later put it, "Even though I had asked them to do it, I was traumatized when my secretary got up and left me in midyell. By the second day, if I so much as raised my voice, whoever was in my office would start to stand up. I would feel momentarily pissed because we were in the middle of working out some important plan or other, and then I'd remember and shut up for a minute. After a while it started to get silly. Anytime anyone stood up—to get some coffee, take off a sweater, anything—I'd stare and then we'd both break up. I'll tell you, it was the greatest team-building move I ever made. Now I've got my kids at home doing it, and we have more peace and quiet than any home inhabited by two teenagers ought to have."

10

The Pros and Cons of Going Deeper

Murray Rose was referred to me by the corporate human resources vice president, who made sure that I knew that the real impetus for the referral came from the CEO. "The fact is," I was told, "Dale, the CEO, is getting pressure from his executive staff to dump Murray."

It was not an unusual story. Murray was the director of research for an upwardly propelled high-tech company. Although his group was alleged to have wasted large sums on projects that never came to fruition, it was also true that the group's single, brilliantly conceived technical breakthrough had given the corporation a two-year lead over its competition. Even his enemies had to admit that the bottom-line balance for Murray and his researchers was well in the black. The real problem was Murray.

Curtis Hamilton, operations senior vice president and Murray's major nemesis, described him thus: "Rose is a mental whiz, no question of that, but he's also a mental case. Yeah, I know that's not very nice, but it's more than that.

He's disorganized and defensive. Yesterday, for instance, he presented his preview of new products to the executive group. I'd spotted some unrealistic cost projections—he just hadn't done his homework—and the next thing I knew he was screaming at me, pounding the table, and accusing me of being a reactionary dinosaur. Dale finally had to call a break and practically sit on him to get through the rest of the meeting. He does this too often, and I, for one, don't want to put up with it anymore. He's smart, but he never should have been made vice president."

Although they were neither as willing to be blunt as Curtis nor as cruel in their judgments, Murray's other colleagues told much the same story. Murray, recognizing that his fervent defenses were jeopardizing his job, agreed to show his good faith (and get the CEO off of his back) by working systematically at moderating his behavior.

One year later, just as I'd just finished interviewing Curtis, Murray's bitterest enemy, on a different matter, he smiled and said, "What did you do to Murray, Doc? What I mean is, he hasn't ranted at me for six months now. He even seems better organized—or maybe he just lets his people organize him better—but I'm impressed. Maybe I ought to let you work on me."

He was correct that Murray had indeed altered important aspects of his behavior. While it had not been easy for him, he had worked tenaciously at each step of his program. He had substituted a demand for explication ("All right, let me hear your reasons") when criticized for his previous cut-and-rip pattern ("You're too stupid to understand"), and as Curtis had guessed, he had allowed his better-organized staff to take him in hand. So I was surprised when Murray called, shortly after Curtis's complimentary comment.

"Dr. Bramson," he said, sounding a little tense even over the phone, "can you give me the name of a good therapist, someone I could work with? Getting a handle on my temper helped me a lot, but I wonder about going deeper."

"What goals did you have in mind?" I asked.

"Does it make a difference? Well, I have three reasons. First off, I was intrigued by those discussions we had about how I seemed to think I should always know the answer to every question or else I'm no good. I'm wondering what else about my thinking might be screwed up. Then there's Rema, the woman I've been seeing. She keeps pushing me to be more open about myself, and I'm having problems with it, at least according to her." He was silent for a time.

"You said three reasons," I ventured.

"It's my son," he started, "I . . . it's just that I yell at him a lot, like I did at work. He doesn't seem all that upset by it, but the thing is, I feel really angry a lot of the time, even when I'm not yelling."

Like Murray, at some point you may wonder about going deeper, about whether your efforts at managing your troublesome behavior might usefully be buttressed by counseling, therapy, guidance, or support from others, in addition to that garnered from your family or immediate coworkers. For Murray, the answer was yes. Several months later, the therapist to whom I had referred him called (at Murray's request) for my impressions of him. As we shared thoughts, I learned something of the source of Murray's so easily aroused rage—a rather horrific early life. Should he, I wondered then, have entered therapy before trying to modify his angry outbursts at work?

When I spoke with him briefly two years later, Murray told me that he felt much less angry most of the time. It would have been an easier road all along if he had felt then as he did now. On the other hand, he said, if he hadn't learned to manage his behavior then, he probably would have been fired, and it would have been a devastating experience for him. He might never have gone into therapy without the encouragement of discovering that he could change things for the better.

"I suppose the best alternative," he said at the end, "would have been to have done both at the same time. How come you didn't suggest that when we first talked?"

"Well," I replied, "at the time your goals were to stop being so disruptive, to get Curtis off your back, and to not get fired. To reach them, you certainly needed to change your behavior, but not necessarily your psyche. But an even more important question is, 'Were you ready then for the therapy experience you've had over the past two years?' Maybe you were and I missed it."

Thus far the focus of this book has been outward (how you, as you are, can reduce the harmful effects of your troublesome behaviors), rather than inward (how you might remediate the underlying causes of those behaviors). I've tried to stay with this focus for several reasons.

First, because the same attribute can be put to both positive and negative uses, it's very possible to turn a liability into a strength without much change in your personality. Similarly, it is usually not necessary to understand yourself better to manage your behavior. Nor does self-understanding always lead to better behavior, although it often does.

Second, changing your behavior will, over time, change the way others treat you, and that, in turn, will alter your own view of the kind of person you are. When that happens, you will indeed have become a different person.

Third, as I suggested to Murray, an inward search will be of greatest value to you only when you are strongly motivated to feel differently, as well as behave differently; and it is certainly possible to display behaviors that put others off and still feel little psychic pain. If this is the case for you, you're unlikely to put yourself through the often arduous emotional work that accompanies a journey of self-discovery. Of course, the opposite is true. You may show only the most trivial behavioral flaws and yet feel emotionally overwhelmed. Although your friends and coworkers may wonder why you are going to all that bother, you may feel very sure of your need for psychotherapy or other developmental experiences.

With this background in mind, the following criteria may help you to decide whether going deeper is for you.

INDICATORS THAT SUPPLEMENTAL THERAPEUTIC EFFORTS MIGHT BE OF VALUE TO YOU

- You have not yet been able to start yourself on a behavior-management program. While you know that your behavior liabilities seem to rankle the people that count, you hold back because it still seems to you that it might be the frustrating people or situations that you've encountered that make you appear difficult.

- Powerful or insistent feelings and impulses keep blocking your attempts to moderate your behavior.

- Your behavior-modification efforts have succeeded reasonably well, but rather than feeling buoyant and relieved, you feel anxious or depressed.

- Your behavior-management efforts have paid off, but you're experiencing one or two of the following signs of harmful stress overload that last for more than two weeks:

  —disturbance in your digestive system
  —rapid increase in pulse or heartbeat not brought on by exercise, sex, or reading Stephen King
  —difficulty in falling or staying asleep
  —feeling tired in the morning
  —tightness in neck, arm, or shoulder muscles or an increase in nail biting, facial tics, or other nervous habits
  —difficulty in focusing your thoughts or unusual forgetfulness about things you usually remember
  —an increase in moodiness or general irritability
  —changes in your use of alcohol or other drugs or in eating habits
  —loss of interest in ordinary pleasures, including sex

- You have made several efforts at managing your target behaviors, had early success, but keep slipping back. You're not sure why, but you are not content with this result. (That is, you don't really *want* to continue being supernice but indecisive—or spontaneous but temperamental.)

- As the result of your successful efforts, you've become curious about why you behave as you do, and you'd like to find out more, although your curiosity may be tempered by some apprehension about what you will find.

There are many reasons for undertaking psychotherapy, and people are so complicated and diverse that there is no developmental approach that works well for everyone. On the other hand, because there is such a diversity of approaches, there does seem to be a growth process that will be right for anyone ready to engage in it. An important first step is to think hard about your specific reasons for going deeper and to have some rather clear goals in mind.

Let's say that "micromanager" is the label that is holding you back, but, overwhelmed by anxiety that you might be responsible for a less than perfect job, you keep undercutting your attempts at delegation. If so, your therapeutic goal might be to feel less anxious about perfection. Understanding *why* you feel so anxious might be a necessary step along the way, or it might not.

On the other hand, you might be interested in *why,* just because you find yourself so fascinating and want to know even more. In that case, you would list "understanding myself better" as one of your goals. Identifying your therapeutic goals is important, because knowing what you want and don't want from therapy will help you locate the approach that is most likely to help you reach your goals at a cost—in time and money—that you're willing to pay.

In the next few pages I've briefly described four approaches to counseling and therapy that have usefully supplemented behavior-management programs. They are all based on the assumptions that your major goal is smoothing rough behavioral edges, that you have already made consistent efforts to reach that goal, and that you're not sure whether something additional might be indicated.

The list begins with behavior therapy, which focuses almost exclusively on your behavior and the circumstances surrounding it, and ends with what are known as the dynamic psychotherapies, which are mostly inner focused—that is, they help you understand and retrofit the emotional forces that influence your behavior. Since most therapists do tend to label themselves, the best way to find out which approach a particular therapist emphasizes is to ask. However, keep in mind that many therapists are rather eclectic about it all and draw upon many approaches for what they believe will best serve their clients.

THERAPIES THAT ENHANCE BEHAVIOR-CHANGE PROGRAMS

Behavior Therapy

Behavior therapists will help you to set specific goals for your change program and point out how you may have been rewarding, or reinforcing (their term), the very actions that you now say you want to avoid. They have a well-established track record of assisting many clients to gain control over their wayward behaviors, but they are not at all interested in the mental or emotional background underlying the behavior. Active work with such a therapist may last from several months to one year.

Cognitive Therapies

Cognitive therapists believe that it is not what you don't know that gets you into trouble but the nonsense that you are absolutely certain about. They help you pull into full consciousness unrealistic or irrational beliefs that you absorbed as a child, then push you to test those beliefs against the evidence of your less naïve adult mind and experience.

For example, suppose that it's your unrealistic belief that "I have a right to be helped, and if those in authority don't help me, they're terrible people" that moves you to fury when your boss ignores your problems. Your therapist will work with you—and some will work *on* you—to reframe that absolutist belief, sorting the sense from the nonsense, into statements such as "It's nice to get help when I want it, but I don't really *need* it, because if my boss were suddenly to disappear, I could still function. And what do I really mean when I say I have a 'right' to be helped? Yes, my boss often hasn't been helpful, and in part it's because he's incompetent—that's an annoyance—but it doesn't mean that he's a terrible person who deserves to be punished."

Cognitive therapy may be particularly apt for you if you are of a contemplative nature, that is, if you prefer to think about your feelings and talk about them rather than directly express them. Cognitive therapists may describe themselves as such, or as cognitive-behavioral therapists, or they may use the term "rational emotive therapy," a particular variety of cognitive therapy developed by psychologist Albert Ellis. The duration of this therapy can vary greatly, but when the therapeutic goals are limited, it is often concluded in six months or less.

Systemic Brief Therapy

In spite of its forbidding name, this approach to solving problems is fascinatingly simple in concept: when we run into trouble with ourselves or with others, we do whatever seems logical, rational, and sensible to improve the situation, and most of the time it works. If, however, our initial efforts don't do the job, we try again with the same wrong solution or one that differs only in minor particulars, but this time we do it louder, longer, or with embellishments. Since we are still figuratively rubbing the cat's fur the wrong way, these renewed efforts make the problem worse. The way out of this self-defeating cycle is to replace the old, unsuccessful solution with one that is radically different.

That's where the therapists come in. Not being a part of the vicious circle, they can better see the faulty premises that you have been logically pursuing and suggest alternate paths that you have not been able to see. If you see a resemblance between this approach and the use of some of the substitute behaviors in earlier chapters, it is not accidental. Systemic brief therapists usually plan to complete their interventions in five or fewer visits.

Dynamic Psychotherapies

This collection of therapies focuses on helping you understand and reexperience the emotional forces (or, as these therapists may refer to them, the underlying dynamics) that most affect your behavior. Their fundamental precept is that personality change is enabled by an open, honest relationship with another caring human being whose only purpose is to help you. On the way to establishing this relationship, it is expected that you will gain understanding of how previous—and possibly convoluted—relationships with other key people in your life may have left you emotionally vulnerable and laden with troublesome defensive behaviors.

Dynamic therapists vary in the degree to which they will emphasize the value of understanding the twists and turns of your psyche, but with or without that intellectual background, if all goes well, you can expect a lessening of emotional storms, tensions, and anxieties.

The dynamic psychotherapies can be long term (years) or short term (but at least six months), and practitioners may profess one of many different conceptual rationales. However, regardless of their theoretical bents, the good ones mostly do and say very similar things. This approach may be the most suitable for you if you have high levels of anxiety or if you have an emotionally expressive nature.

OTHER KINDS OF HELP THAT ARE NOT EXACTLY THERAPY

Twelve-Step Groups

The best known twelve-step group is Alcoholics Anonymous, but there are currently many others with similar formats that center their programs on a variety of hard to manage behaviors. Among the strengths of these programs are an unremitting acceptance in the face of repeated slips and slides and a normalizing of troublesome behavior. The message is, "We've all been there; you're not alone." Consequently, they are particularly helpful to those who have many times failed to manage their problem behavior and are despondent about being able to change.

The twelve-step programs that have been formally evaluated (mostly AA) show success rates equal to those of more conventional therapeutic methods if the sole criterion is the degree to which the unwanted behavior is brought under control. In urban areas, you should be able to find a program that is at least tangentially related to your work problem. Anger, codependency, and relationship-addiction groups are all programs that have aided clients who value them for their support and encouragement and who return to them as a place to renew commitment.

Living-in-Process Groups

Living-in-Process is the name of a relatively new approach to mutual support and personal development in our disjointed modern society. You can find in these facilitated but nontherapy groups a source of the candid but nonaccusing feedback that is so valuable in pursuing your behavior-change goals, along with a chance to model and practice clear, open communications in a supportive and friendly atmosphere. You may have difficulty in locating a local source, but you can obtain information on groups in your community by writing to Living-in-Process Network, c/o Wilson Schaef Associates, P.O. Box 18686, Boulder, CO 80308.

A PERSONAL NOTE

Well, none of it is very easy, is it? I've always asked the clients who, with some success, have made their way through the labors and rough places that have been the substance of this book—the "obstacle course," as one called it—what enabled them to make it through. Most ruefully attributed their persistence to an inability to forget or otherwise ignore whatever career hindrance had caught their attention in the first place.

"I didn't have an alternative; it was get organized or get fired," some would say, or, "I knew I'd never get back on the promotion track until I got the staff, both blue- and white-collar, behind me," or, "I just got tired of having the worst sales stats in the district." For most, it was a confusing trip. There was almost universal apprehension at looking into the mirror of others' perceptions, the insecurities of behaving unnaturally, and irritation at me for continually poking at them when their reasons turned to rationalizations.

But there were also bursts of joy, as well as some amazement, when their new ways elicited changed behavior in others. They felt renewed confidence in their ability to effect a change in their lives when they needed to, and they saw themselves less as victims or victimizers than as immensely interesting people with fascinating puzzles to solve. As ex-know-it-all Sally—still a force to be reckoned with—put it, "I didn't exactly look forward to the feedback, and some of the rest of it was pretty messy, but hell, how else could I show 'em what I was made of?"

How else, indeed?

Notes

SECTION I

PAGE

14 For one evaluation of a behavior management program as an accompaniment to therapy, see A. Stranyvski, S. Grey, and R. Elie, "Outline of the therapeutic process in social skills training with socially dysfunctional patients," *Journal of Consulting and Clinical Psychology* 55 (1985): 204–28.

CHAPTER 1

PAGE

19 An excellent delineation of the stages characteristic of a change process can be found in J. O. Prochask, C. C. DiClemente, and J. C. Norcross, "In search of how people change," *American Psychologist* 47 (1992): 1102–14.

19–20 My descriptions of the vagaries of underachievers reflect my professional experience with technically proficient blue- and white-collar workers. For a broader view, see J. J. Gallagher, "Personal patterns of underachievement," *Journal for the Education of the Gifted* 14 (1991): 221–33.

20–21 A. Tesser, "The importance of heritability in psychological research: the case of attitudes," *Psychological Review* 100, no. 1 (1993): 129–42.

For a relatively nontechnical discussion of genetic determinants of behavior, see L. A. Baker and R. Clark, eds., "Genetic origins of behavior: Implications for counselors," *Journal of Counseling and Development* 68 (1990).

For a more technical review, see L. Willerman and J. M. Horn, "Human behavior genetics," *Annual Review of Psychology* (1988): 101–33.

A nicely evenhanded review of the evidence for inherited aggressive tendencies is to be found in J. Keegan, *A History of Warfare* (New York: Knopf, 1993).

22–23 K. Gergen, *The Saturated Self: Dilemmas of Identity in Contemporary Life* (New York: Basic Books, 1991).

23–24 Feeling in control is the best mitigator of harmful stress; hence the value of choosing to take action because *you* have decided that it is to your benefit. See, for example, E. Langer, "The illusion of control," *Journal of Personality and Social Psychology* 32 (1975): 311–28, and R. F. Baumeister, J. C. Hamilton, and D. M. Tice, "Public versus private expectancy of success: Confidence booster or personality pressure?" *Journal of Personality and Social Psychology* 48 (1985): 1447–57.

27 A. Tversky and D. Kahneman, "Rational choice and the framing of decisions," *Journal of Business* 59 (1986): 251–94.

CHAPTER 2

PAGE

34 In outlining the reasons why we often misread others' views of ourselves, I've drawn on many resources. The most important: D. A. Kenny and B. M. DePaulo, "Do people know how others view them? An empirical and theoretical account," *Psychological Bulletin* 114 (1993): 145–61; M. R. Leary, *Understanding Social Anxiety* (Newberry Park, Cal.: Sage, 1993); B. Weiner, "On sin versus sickness: A theory or perceived responsibility and social motivation," *American Psychologist* 48 (1993): 957–65; H. Tennen and G. Affleck, "Blaming others for threatening events," *Psychological Bulletin* 108 (1990): 209–32; A. G. Greenwald, "The totalitarian ego: Fabrication and revision of personal history," *American Psychologist* 35 (1980): 603–18; S. E. Taylor and J. D. Brown, "Illusion and well-being: A social psychological perspective on mental health," *Psychological Bulletin* 103 (1988): 193–210; S. E. Taylor, *Positive Illusions* (New York: Basic Books, 1990); and J. D. Brown, "Self-esteem and self-evaluation: Feeling is believing," in *Psychological Perspectives on the Self*, vol. 4, edited by J. Suls (Hillsdale, N. J.: Erlbaum, 1993), 27–58.

36 For a discussion of the strength-weakness paradox as it applies to cognitive style, see A. F. Harrison and R. M. Bramson, *The Art of Thinking* (New York: Berkley Books, 1984) and J. D. W. Andrews, "Integrating visions of reality: Interpersonal diagnosis and the existential vision," *American Psychologist* 44: 803–17.

37 For suggestions on clarifying expectations with bosses, you might check my *Coping with Difficult Bosses* (New York: Fireside Books/Simon & Schuster, 1994), 116–24.

39 S. Seligman, *Learned Optimism* (New York: Knopf, 1991), chapter 5.

39 C. Garfield, *Peak Performers* (New York: William Morrow, 1986).

40 If most of us are so blind to the impressions that we make on others, how do we manage to build well-integrated teams? One rather disturbing answer to that question is that much of the time we don't. The work (or sports) groups we call teams depend on some outside coordinating mechanism in the form of a coach, a team captain, or a set of roles, policies, and procedures to regulate behavior. In fact, recent studies show that attaining truly interactive teamwork requires an enormous amount of training and mutually examined experience. Even then, misreadings, frightfully wrong assumptions, and miscommunications frequently occur and need to be ironed out. Interestingly, most of us no longer hold illusions about the ease of maintaining relationships at home; witness the proliferation of popular books and magazine pieces on how better to stay in tune with spouses, children, or significant others.

43 The 20 percent figure comes from unpublished data developed in our studies of difficult people in organizational settings.

45 For a conceptual/experimental treatment of why it's often difficult to obtain negative feedback from others, see A. Tesser and S. Rosen, "The reluctance to transmit bad news," in *Advances in Experimental Social Psychology,* vol. 8, edited by L. Berkowitz (1975): 194–232.

49 Susan Bramson provided invaluable help in delineating the various approaches to obtaining feedback described on pages 42–58.

54 For further explication on why informants may disagree, see D. A. Kenny, L. Albright, T. E. Malloy, and D. A. Kashy, "Consensus in interpersonal perception: Acquaintance and the big five," *Psychological Bulletin* 116 (1994): 245–58, and R. Saavedra and S. K. Kwun, "Peer evaluation in self-managing work groups," *Journal of Applied Psychology* 78 (1993): 450–62.

55 For more suggestions on how to make use of negative feedback (as well as how to usefully give it), try H. Weisinger, *The Critical Edge: How to Criticize Up and Down Your Organization and Make It Pay Off* (Boston: Little, Brown, 1989).

57 The notion of reframing thoughts and perceptions to avoid self-defeating feedback loops is essential to most cognitive therapies. For various approaches to this process, see L. P. Rehm and P. Rokke, "Self-management therapies," and R. J. DeRubeis and A. T. Beck, "Cognitive therapy," in *Handbook of Cognitive-Behavioral Therapies,* edited by K. S. Dobson (New York: Gilford Press, 1988). For a more popular exposition of another approach to cognitive therapy, see A. Ellis and A. Lange, *How to Keep People from Pushing Your Buttons* (New York: Birch Lane Press, 1994).

58 For a recent review of studies on the relationship of gender and self-assessment in work settings, see T. Roberts, "Gender and the influence of evaluations on self-assessments in achievement settings," *Psychological Bulletin* 109 (1991): 297–308.

60–61 R. Bandler and J. Grinder, *Frogs into Princes* (Moab, Utah: Real People Press, 1979).

CHAPTER 3

PAGE

64–65 When you commit your plan to paper, you are in effect writing a new story about the person you might be. You not only crystalize a new way of behaving but enfold it into the realities of your capabilities, goals, and environment. For more on the power of visualizing a possible self, see H. Markus, and P. Nurius, "Possible Selves," *American Psychologist* 41 (1986): 954–69.

65 See, for example, the extensive literature on commitment to change in organizations; for example, B. M. Steaw and J. Ross, "Behavior in escalation situations: Antecedents, prototypes, and solutions," in *Research in Organizational Behavior,* vol. 9, edited by L. L. Cummings and B. M. Steaw (Greenwich, Conn.: J A I Press, 1987), 39–78.

65–66 For amplification of the value of recalling slippery situations in which you behaved well, see C. W. H. O'Hanlon and M. Weiner-Davis, *In Search of Solutions* (New York: Norton, 1989), and S. deShazer, *Keys to Solution in Brief Therapy* (New York: Norton, 1985).

67 In R. Fisch, J. H. Weakland, and L. Segal, *The Tactics of Change: Doing Therapy Briefly* (San Francisco: Jossey-Bass, 1982), are examples of the trouble-provoking effects of one up, one down interactions.

69–70 For an up-to-date summary of current thinking on multiple routes to the emotions, see C. E. Izard, "Four systems for emotional activation: Cognitive and noncognitive processes," *Psychological Review* 100 (1993): 68–90. For other points of view, see R. B. Zajonc, "Feeling and thinking: Preferences need no inferences," *American Psychologist* 35 (1980): 151–75, and R. S. Lazarus, "Cognition and motivation in emotion," *American Psychologist* 46 (1991): 352–67.

72 For discussions of how people cope with stress in the workplace, see A. Monat and R. S. Lazarus, eds., *Stress and Coping: An Anthology* (New York: Columbia University Press, 1985), and M. T. Matteson and J. M. Ivancevich, *Controlling Work Stress* (San Francisco: Jossey-Bass, 1987).

72 For a cogent and lively discussion of individualized responses to physical settings, see A. Mehrabian, *Public Places and Private Spaces: The Psychology of Work, Play, and Living Environments* (New York: Basic Books, 1976).

74 Although Argyris has argued that commanded participation can lead to confusion—see C. Argyris, *Strategy, Change and Defensive Routines* (Boston: Pitman, 1985)—I have found that this approach works well if the reasons for it are clearly stated and the boss feels as bound by the requirement for open communication as do the team members.

74 For an excellent literature review on nonverbal behavior, see B. M. DePaulo, "Nonverbal behavior and self-presentation," *Psychological Bulletin* 3 (1992): 203–43, and, of course, Ervin Goffman's classic *The Presentation of Self in Everyday Life* (Garden City, N. Y.: Doubleday/Anchor Books, 1959).

77 Labeling a sarcastic remark as such, in a nonattacking way, removes much of its sting; people react less to your behavior than to the meaning they ascribe to it.

78 For more on skillful role presentations, see, for example, R. E. Riggio and H. S. Friedman, "Impression formation: The role of expressive behavior," *Journal of Personality and Social Psychology* 50: 421–27, and P. J. DePaulo and B. M. DePaulo, "Can attempted deception by salespersons and customers be detected through nonverbal behavioral cues?" *Journal of Applied Social Psychology* 19 (1989): 1552–57.

CHAPTER 4

PAGE

87 For a more extensive discussion of breaking a task into smaller, more manageable steps, see my *Coping with the Fast-Track Blues* (New York: Dell, 1992), 90–95.

88 For a nontechnical review of the evidence for imagery and mental

practice, see J. Amnett, "The learning of motor skills: Sports science and ergonomics perspectives," *Ergonomics* 37 (1994): 5–16.

89 The stepwise behavior-control method is consistent with a number of widely based therapeutic approaches, namely problem-solving therapies (see, for example, T. J. D'Zurilla, *Problem-Solving Therapy: A Social Competence Approach to Clinical Intervention* [New York: Springer, 1986]) and self-management therapies (for an excellent summary of this approach, see L. P. Rehm and P. Rokke, "Self-Management Therapies," in *Handbook of Cognitive-Behavioral Therapies,* edited by K. S. Dobson [New York: Guilford Press, 1988]).

90–91 Physical cuing is an attention-refocusing device that has proved its worth in behavior therapy. For a broad and integrated view of current thoughts on behavioral therapy, see A. W. Staats, "Psychological behaviorism: An overarching theory and a theory-construction methodology," *The General Psychologist* 29 (1993): 46–60.

98 For a simplified discussion of screening levels as it applies to family interactions, see R. M. Bramson and S. Bramson, *The Stressless Home* (New York: Ballantine Books, 1986). For a more thorough discussion, see A. Mehrabian, *Public Place and Private Spaces: The Psychology of Work, Play, and Living Environments* (cited previously).

98–99 For more on perfectionism, see R. O. Frost, P. Marten, C. Lahart, and R. Rosenblate, "The dimensions of perfectionism," *Cognitive Therapy and Research* 14 (1990): 449–68.

99 A. Ellis and W. Dryden, *The Practice of Rational-Emotive Therapy* (New York: Springer, 1987).

100–101 One point on which both Freudians and behaviorists agree is that people learn behavioral tendencies because in some way they satisfy. I've never found much to contradict Freud's conclusion (paraphrased) that "every problem is also a satisfaction."

101 There is ample evidence that behavioral control is eroded during times of high emotional arousal. See, for example, H. Heckhausen and J. Beckmann, "Intentional action and action slips," *Psychological Review* 97 (1990): 36–48.

104 An interesting discussion of the benefits that accrue when therapists take a one-down position is to be found in R. Fisch, J. Weakland, and L. Segal, *The Tactics of Change: Doing Therapy Briefly* (previously cited), 34–35.

108 Some people monitor themselves all the time, matching their performance against some inner standard. While this self-conscious quality can be burdensome when one is trying for spontaneity, it does minimize straying too far off course, an important consideration when the pitfalls are many.

109 One of the best practical manuals on communicating assertively is still M. Burley-Allen, *Managing Assertively: How to Improve Your People Skills* (New York: Wiley, 1983).

CHAPTER 5

PAGE

112　For a review of the literature on impression management (the general topic under which image changing is studied), see M. R. Leary and R. M. Kowalsky, "Impression management: A literature review and two-component model," *Psychological Bulletin* 107 (1990): 34–47.

114　For reviews of the advantages and disadvantages of stereotypic thinking, see, for example, D. T. Gilbert and J. G. Hickson, "The trouble of thinking: Activation and application of stereotypic belief," *Journal of Personality and Social Psychology* 60 (1991): 509–17; S. B. Gurwitz and K. A. Dodge, "Effects of confirmations and disconfirmations on stereotype-based attributions," *Journal of Personality and Social Psychology* 35 (1977): 495–500; E. A. Hogan, "Effects of prior expectations on performance ratings: A longitudinal study," *Academy of Management Journal* 30 (1987): 354–68; and E. Langer, A. Blank, and B. Chanowitz, "The mindlessness of ostensibly thoughtful action: The role of 'placebic' information in interpersonal interaction," *Journal of Personality and Social Psychology* 36 (1978): 635–42.

116　For an interesting confirmation of the fact that some images change slowly as a result of repeated exposure to the person who has changed, while others resist change until an unusual event has forced it, see P. J. Hanges and E. P. Braverman, "Changes in raters' perceptions of subordinates: A catastrophe model," *Journal of Applied Psychology* 76 (1991): 878–88.

116　The efficacy of this method for impression management first came to my attention when I was a young infantryman undergoing that brand of torture called basic training. A fellow sufferer, wise beyond his years, having privately announced his intention to a few of us, maneuvered a transfer out of the infantry by limping painfully on hikes and other exercises while bravely refusing all attempts at succor from initially suspicious and then sympathetic drill sergeants. His adamantly uncomplaining refusal to be relieved from duty was so contrary to the picture of the stereotypical malingerer that the training cadre became convinced that he was in fact incapable of surviving as an infantryman. I later read a similar, if more ethical, use of the same method by a concentration camp inmate, a psychologist who kept his emotional balance by observing the phenomena of what was happening to him and his fellow inmates. He was able to obtain badly needed medical treatment for himself by initially refusing medical aid, thereby disconfirming his guard's stereotype of his ethnic group as cowardly, whining complainers. Thus far, about twelve of my clients who found themselves in situations similar to Nicole's have ethically used this approach to good effect.

117　For more on the need for control in impression management, see D. M. Wegner and R. Erber, "Social foundations of mental control," in *Handbook of Mental Control,* edited by D. M. Wegner (Englewood Cliffs, N. J.: Prentice-Hall, 1993).

118　For a recent discussion of the advantages of becoming skillful in impression management (as well as guidelines for those on the receiving end of it), see W. L. Gardner, "Lessons in organizational dramaturgy: The art of impression management," *Organizational Dynamics* 21 (1992): 33–46.

CHAPTER 6

PAGE

126　For further explication on the problems that hardheads and hard-noses can cause, you might see my *Coping with Difficult People* (New York: Dell, 1988), 9–42, 113–36.

127　In this and the succeeding chapters, I've tried to stay with descriptors of motivations and satisfactions as they appear in consciousness, since that's the material that you, the one embarking on the change process, can work with.

128　Seventy-four percent of the participants in two seminars on Coping with Difficult People said they would prefer "I need to insist" over "Do it." Reasons given included "more personal," "less abrupt," "just more courteous." Client reports over the years bear out that the wording makes a difference. One probable reason for this is the subtle suggestion from the words "I need to . . ." that the demand for compliance stems not from a personal need to exercise power but from some external circumstance. That notion is consonant with findings that anger is much less likely to follow when an act is seen as outside the control of the actor. See, for example, J. R. Averill, "Studies in anger and aggression," *American Psychologist* 38 (1983): 1145–60, and B. Weiner, *An Attributional Theory of Management and Emotion* (New York: Springer, 1986).

130　For a brief literature review and an example of research that confirms the wisdom of enforced reflectivity on aggressively extrovertive individuals, see C. M. Patterson, D. S. Kosson, and J. P. Newman, "Reaction to punishment, reflectivity, and passive avoidance learning in extroverts," *Journal of Personality and Social Psychology* 52: 565–75.

CHAPTER 7

PAGE

134　Carl was an interesting example of how one can hold seemingly contradictory attitudes when occupational roles interact with different aspects of the same innate or early-learned tendencies. Although he was certainly an overly permissive manager, his colleagues thought him rather punitive when dealing with their criminal quarry. Incompetence was to be lived with, but dishonesty was evidently beyond the pale. The opposite effect, of course, is often seen in the autocratic and uncaring manner in which many labor union employees are treated.

135　For a fuller examination of the relationship of personality attributes to decision-making difficulties, see J. R. Ferrari, "Decisional procrastination: Examining personality correlates," *Journal of Personality and Social Behavior* 4 (1989): 151–61.

Further explication of the behavior and motivation of those who are too helpful or too caring can be found in my *Coping with Difficult People*, 85–98, 137–58.

138   Because they put the responsibility for limit setting on the requirements of your job or your business, these substitute behaviors are consistent with findings that your actions are less likely to provoke anger when they are seen as caused by external events. See, for example, B. Weiner, "On sin versus sickness: The theory of perceived responsibility and social motivation" (previously cited), 957–65.

CHAPTER 8

PAGE

143   For an article that points out the value of complaining when done well, see F. J. Crosby, "Why complain?" *Journal of Social Issues* 49 (1993): 169–84.

In 1978, Avraham Zamir, an immensely creative Israeli entrepreneur, pointed out to me the invaluable contribution that those with a negativist bent can make to decision-making discussions. He also emphasized the importance of distinguishing between negatives as potential problems to be planned around and negatives as reasons to abort a decision.

145   For additional perspectives on complaining and negativism, see my *Coping with Difficult People*, 43–68, 99–112.

CHAPTER 9

PAGE

150   You can get more information on why tears happen in work settings from J. M. Plas and K. V. Hoover-Dempsey, *Working Up a Storm: Anger, Anxiety, Joy, and Tears on the Job* (New York: Norton, 1988), 112–75.

I believe the best popular book on anger is still C. Tavris, *Anger: The Misunderstood Emotion* (New York: Simon & Schuster, 1984).

For a brief but informative guide for professionals on treating anger problems from the rational-emotive perspective, see W. Dryden, *Dealing with Anger Problems* (Sarasota, Fla.: Professional Resources Exchange, 1990). (Write to P.O. Box 15560, Sarasota, FL 34277.)

155   Most people can discern the unrealistic elements of some of their early-learned beliefs once they've accepted the notion that those rules for living aren't immutable—they can be questioned. In fact, simply *trying* to differentiate the sense from the nonsense weakens the power of those "should's." In *How to Keep People from Pushing Your Buttons* (previously cited), Ellis and Lange lead their readers through just such an untangling process.

CHAPTER 10

160 For example, Rodney Lowman has pointed out that in response to workplace pressures, even those with severe personality problems can learn to manage their behavior better. See R. L. Lowman, *Counseling and Psychotherapy of Work Dysfunctions* (Washington, D.C.: American Psychological Association, 1993), 184.

160 For an intriguing discussion of the way in which others' reactions affect one's view of oneself, see H. Markus and P. Nurius, "Possible selves," *American Psychologist* 41 (1986): 954–69.

161 For a collection of somewhat disjointed but informative articles on stress and its workplace effects, see A. Monat and R. S. Lazarus, eds., *Stress and Coping: An Anthology* (New York: Columbia University Press, 1985).

161 Although most psychotherapists would agree that certain kinds of therapy are more or less suitable for particular patients and particular problems, it has been difficult to get objective evidence to demonstrate that. There is strong and robust evidence that most people are helped by psychotherapy, but overall, one variety seems about as effective as the other. Given the diversity of human beings and their problems, however, it is probable that the difficulty lies in inappropriate research designs and inadequate measurement tools. For more on this topic, see W. B. Stiles, D. A. Shapiro, and R. Elliott, "Are all psychotherapies equivalent?" *American Psychologist* 41 (1986): 165–80.

   For a recent review of the efficacy of psychological treatment in general, see M. W. Lipsey and D. B. Wilson, "The efficacy of psychological, educational, and behavioral treatment: A confirmation from meta-analysis," *American Psychologist* 48 (1993): 1181–1209.

162 The difference between counseling and psychotherapy is more formal or legal than substantive. Many states have legally restricted psychotherapy to psychiatrists, clinical psychologists, and licensed clinical social workers. Other practitioners, however, licensed or certified as marriage and family counselors, mental-health nurses, or as other mental-health professionals must restrict their practice to "counseling." In actuality, what they all do and how well they do it depends more on their inclination, knowledge, and skill than on their occupational titles.

162 For a fuller description of eclectic psychotherapy, see, for example, L. E. Beutler, *Eclectic Psychotherapy: A Systematic Approach* (New York: Pergamon, 1983).

163 Most behavioral therapists write for other behavioral therapists, not their potential clients, but see J. E. Mazur, *Learning and Behavior* (Englewood Cliffs, N.J.: Prentice Hall, 1990), and M. J. Mahoney, *Human Change Processes* (New York: Basic Books, 1990).

163 For more on cognitive therapy, see any of the previously cited texts, for example, K. T. Kuehwein and H. Rosen, eds., *Cognitive Therapies in Action: Evolving Innovative Practice,* or Keith Dobson's *Handbook of Cognitive-Behavioral Therapies.*

164   Unfortunately, there is not yet a book or article for the layperson on brief systemic therapy, but see S. deShazer, *Keys to Solution in Brief Therapy* (New York: Norton, 1985), and R. Fisch, J. H. Weakland, and L. Segal, *The Tactics of Change: Doing Therapy Briefly* (previously cited).

For an interesting approach that combines both cognitive and brief systemic therapy, see C. H. Huber and B. A. Backlund, *The Twenty-Minute Counselor: Transforming Brief Conversations into Effective Helping Experiences* (New York: Continuum, 1992).

164   Although most authorities use the term "dynamic psychotherapy" as a synonym for psychoanalytically oriented therapy, I use it here in a much broader context. While the other approaches I've mentioned focus solely on behavior, or on the way you think about yourself and your situation, or on the situational context of the problem, dynamic therapies purport to reconstitute and reintegrate the various aspects of your personality. Two recent discussions of dynamic therapies that might be of a special interest to the readers of this book are P. L. Wachtel's *Action and Insight* (New York: Guilford, 1987), a fascinating attempt to integrate the psychoanalytic approach with behavior therapy, and Jim Bugental's dynamic approach to existential-humanistic psychotherapy, which connects both the reality of experience and the deeper mysteries of inner life—*Intimate Journeys: Stories from Life-Changing Therapy* (San Francisco: Jossey-Bass, 1990).

165   My belief that competent therapists tend not to differ much in what they actually say and do comes from the opportunities I've had to colead groups with therapists of quite different persuasions, from my own therapeutic experiences, and from conversations with therapists to whom I've referred clients. However, my thoughts were first set in this direction by M. A. Lieberman, I. D. Yalom, and M. B. Miles, *Encounter Groups: First Facts* (New York: Basic Books, 1973). That interesting study of encounter groups confirmed my own earlier observations that, although group leaders often professed widely diverse therapeutic orientations, those who facilitated groups that were judged to have led to the most learning and change tended to do very much the same things.

165   Well-designed evaluations of the comparative effectiveness of self-help groups in general and twelve-step groups in particular are yet to be done. For rather positive reviews of the current relationship between these methods and more traditional approaches, see M. Lieberman, "Self-help groups and psychiatry," *American Psychiatric Association Annual Review* 5 (1986): 744–69, and M. K. Jacobs and G. Goodman, "Psychology and self-help groups: Predictions on a partnership," *American Psychologist* 44 (1989): 536–45.

165   For a description of Living-in-Process groups, see A. W. Schaef, *Beyond Therapy, Beyond Science: A New Model for Healing the Whole Person* (San Francisco: Harper Collins, 1992). While I disagree with her rather critical view of psychotherapy, I believe the Living-in-Process method has much to commend it.